Precious Essence

Precious Essence

The Inner Autobiography of
Terchen Barway Dorje

Translated by

Yeshe Gyamtso

KTD Publications
Woodstock, New York USA

Published by:
KTD Publications
335 Meads Mountain Road
Woodstock, NY 12498 USA
www.KTDPublications.org

Distributed by:
Namse Bangdzo Bookstore
335 Meads Mountain Road
Woodstock, NY 12498 USA
www.NamseBangdzo.com

ISBN 0-9741092-5-8

This book is printed on acid free paper.

Contents

THE KARMAPA

༄༅། །པདྨའི་རྗེ་འབངས་ཉེར་ལྔའི་ཡ་གྱལ་གནུབས་སངས་རྒྱས་ཀྱི་སྐྱེ་བརྒྱུད་གཏེར་འབྱིན་རིན་པོ་ཆེ་འབར་བའི་རྡོ་རྗེ་སྐྱེ་ཕྲེང་དང་པོ་ནི། དུས་རབས་བཅུ་དགུའི་ནང་བོད་དུ་བྱོན་ཅིང་། དུས་རབས་དེར་བྱོན་པའི་དམ་པ་མང་ཞིག་གིས་གཏེར་སྟོན་ཚད་ལྡན་དུ་བཀུར་ཞིང་བསྔགས་པ་དང་། གཏེར་ཆོས་ཀྱང་། རིག་འཛིན་བླ་སྒྲུབ་དང་། ཞུར་པ། མཁའ་འགྲོའི་ཆོས་སྐོར་བཅས་སྨིན་གྲོལ་གྱི་གདམས་ཟབ་མང་ཚན་ཡོད་པ་ལས། ཞུར་པའི་ཆོས་སྐོར་དེར་༧རྒྱལ་དབང་སྐུ་གོང་མ་རིག་པའི་རྡོ་རྗེས་ཐུགས་སྣང་ཤིན་ཏུ་ཆེ། གཞན་ཡང་ཁོང་ཉིད་ཀྱིས་གནང་བའི་འབའ་རོམ་བཀའ་བརྒྱུད་པའི་ཕྱག་ཆེན་དང་ཆོས་དྲུག་སོགས་སྙིང་པོའི་བསྟན་པ་ལ་སྨན་ཡོན་ཆེ་བ་དུ་མ་བཞུགས། ད་ལམ་འདི་ཉིད་ཀྱི་རྣམ་ཐར་བོད་དང་རྒྱ་གར་གཉིས་སུ་བྲིས་མ་མ་དཔེ་གཅིག་རང་བཞུགས་པ་དེར་ཁྲུངས་བཅོལ་ཏེ། དབྱིན་སྐད་དང་རྒྱ་སྐད་གཉིས་སུ་ཕབ་བསྒྱུར་ཞུ་རྒྱུ་དེར་ཡི་རང་དང་། ལེགས་ལམ་འདི་ཉིད་ཀྱིས་སེམས་ཅན་རྣམས་ལ་ཐར་པའི་ས་བོན་འཛུག་པའི་བསྔོ་སྨོན་བྱེད། ཀརྨ་པར་འབོད་པ། ཨོ་རྒྱན་ཕྲིན་ལས་རྡོ་རྗེས། ནང་ལོ་ ༢༥༤༧ ཕྱི་ལོ་ ༢༠༠༣ ཟླ་ ༩ ཚེས་ ༢

The first Barway Dorje was a precious revealer of treasure and the rebirth of Nupchen Sangye Yeshe, one of Guru Padma's twenty-five disciples. Barway Dorje appeared in Tibet during the nineteenth century, and was praised and respected by the many holy beings of his time as an authentic treasure revealer. His many treasures include The Sadhanas of the Vidyadhara Guru, The Vajrakila Cycle, *and* The Dakini Cycle, *all of which contain profound instructions pertaining to ripening and liberation. The previous Gyalwang Karmapa, Rikpe Dorje, displayed great interest in* The Vajrakila Cycle *in particular.*

In addition to his treasures, Terchen Barway Dorje composed many works of his own that have been of great service to the essence teachings, such as his Barom Kagyu Mahamudra *and* Six Doctrines.

One hand-written edition of his biography exists, and is found in both India and Tibet. I am delighted that English and Chinese translations of it are being published, and I make the dedication and aspiration that this good work may plant the seed of liberation in beings.

—Ogyen Trinley Dorje, called "Karmapa," on the second day of September, in the year 2003 of the international calendar, 2587 of the Buddhist calendar.

Terchen Barway Dorje

Translator's Introduction

Dechen Barway Dorje was one of several treasure revealers active at the end of the nineteenth century and the beginning of the twentieth. A disciple of the ninth Tai Situ Rinpoche, of Chokgyur Dechen Lingpa, and of others, Barway Dorje was initially associated with Surmang Monastery. He went on to revive the lost teachings of the Barom Kagyu, and to reveal nine volumes of treasure teachings concealed by Guru Rinpoche, Yeshe Tsogyal, and Nupchen Sangye Yeshe. He was also the reincarnation of both Yeshe Tsogyal and Sangye Yeshe. Toward the end of his life he founded Raktrul Monastery, which is active to this day and has affiliated centers in the United States.

The editor of this autobiography was Kagyu Tashi of Kyodrak Monastery. He was a renowned teacher, scholar, and siddha in his own right, although he adopts a veil of modesty here in his role as a devoted disciple requesting his master to tell of his life and deeds. He became one of the principal holders of the Barom Kagyu teachings of Barway Dorje and of his teachings in general.

This autobiography is actually one of three biographies of Barway Dorje. One is his outer autobiography; one is what is translated here, his inner autobiography; and the third is an account of his funeral observances written by Kagyu Tashi.

The outer autobiography is an extremely modest account of his life in which almost all of his qualities are concealed. The exception is his devotion to his gurus, and in particular to Chokgyur Dechen Lingpa. Barway Dorje initially met this great master when Chokgyur Lingpa married Barway Dorje's sister, Dechen Chödrön. From then on, until Chokgyur Lingpa's death in 1871, Barway Dorje served him continuously.

The inner autobiography, translated here, describes the visionary, inner life of this great treasure revealer. It therefore shows us the wisdom and magnificence of the entire tradition in which Barway Dorje arose. The extraordinary teachings of Barway Dorje are practiced nowadays on both sides of the globe. An understanding of their origin will bring insight into their true value.

Yeshe Gyamtso

This translation is dedicated to
Tenpay Nyima, the Third Bardor Tulku Rinpoche

The Precious Essence

The Hidden Meaning of the Glorious Noble Guru's Life

Devoted homage to the feet of the embodiment of the
three roots—the guru, Vajradhara, Padmakara.[1]

You are the source of liberation as far beyond thought
as space itself.
Possessing the vajra body, you will benefit others through
the play of great bliss as long as space lasts.
Guru, father and mother of peerless kindness, along
with deities, dakinis, and dharmapalas:[2]
One appearing as many—I pay homage by meeting you,
through the view, in the expanse of wisdom.

Embodied result of the supreme path to great awakening,
Holder of the spontaneously perfect, blazing vajra of
great bliss,
Powerful hero, Düdül Lingpa,[3]

Play in the lotus pond of my heart until my awakening.

The vast clouds of your magical display
Are the source of a continuous rain of benefit and bliss.
May you and your children and disciples with mastery
Of great vajra wisdom protect me.

The vajra guru is the treasury of the ocean of qualities
of omniscience,
Extolled as the single gate through which come
The blessings of the three times' victors:
His life is difficult for even the victors to describe properly.
What could be said about this partial attempt by an
infantile mind?
However, with the assurance of pure aspirations from
the past,
I will put forth merely the seeds of his vajra speech.

Here, in order to describe merely the lotus seeds of the inner and secret life of the master of the vast treasury of profound vajra secrets, who will play the music of the deeds of buddhas for as long as space lasts; the protector who, through the unsurpassed conduct of awakening, establishes all the innumerable beings in the state of full liberation; our guide, Guru Mahavajradhara of peerless kindness,[4] there are three parts:

Virtue in the beginning, a description of the circumstances
under which the autobiography was composed;
Virtue in the middle, the actual autobiography;
Virtue in the end, the conclusion of the autobiography.

Virtue in the Beginning

The Circumstances Under Which the Autobiography Was Composed

When the noble guru, the lord of the four bodies, had reached his seventieth year he was abiding in service to the whole doctrine throughout Tibet, in accordance with the command of Guru Rinpoche, the second Buddha, while living at the supreme place of Koro Rock.[5] This was a rock mountain like a vajra pointing into the sky, a place of practice used by Guru Rinpoche, on the banks of the Drichu River, near Singha Dzong in Kham, one of the twenty-five great places in Tibet.

At that time I, who possess the good fortune of having been held in my guru's loving compassion for many lifetimes, being motivated by a genuine wish for the future benefit of the doctrine and beings, impelled by the utterly pure faith and devotion of seeing my guru as an actual buddha, and encouraged by many vajra siblings, offered a substantial mandala and made the following supplication.

Glorious Mahavajradhara in human form,
Peerless father, dharma lion:
I bow to you in non-dual awareness.
Please listen at ease to your son's request.

I bow respectfully with innumerable bodies
And present clouds of Samantabhadra's offerings.
I confess the stains of wrongs done throughout
past lives.
I delight from my heart in your holy deeds.
Send down the rain of mahayana dharma on beings.
Remain permanent and pervasive on the unwavering
throne.
I dedicate, without concepts, whatever virtue there is.

Although my veneration through wealth and goods
is weak,
All the good I will ever do from now until the heart
of awakening
Will be done in your service, my lord.
All my actions will be done to serve you.
Hold me in the regard of your loving mind.

Up there, on the cooling slopes of the mountain,
The white snow lioness abides gracefully.
She has confidence in being undisturbed by her enemy,
the blizzard.
Don't keep that confidence secret; speak of it to me.

Down there, in the slow-flowing river Tsangpo,
The white fish swims in play.

She has the power to move without impediment.
Don't keep that power secret; speak of it to me.

Between them, in the forest of sandalwood,
The man-eating tigress roars.
She has confidence in her own ferocity.
Don't keep that confidence secret; speak of it to me.

In places and lands without limit,
You, the yogin, engaged spontaneously in dual benefit.
You have kept secret and concealed your inconceivable life.
Don't keep it secret; speak of it to me.

For close disciples and subjects,
Bestow an account of your life to engender faith
and devotion.
Through your love, cast us not aside.
Don't conceal it; speak of it to me.

Fill the ladle of this beggar's three-fold faith
With the nectar of your profound speech
So that beings, our mothers, can enjoy it at their pleasure
And be nourished in the attainment of supreme liberation.

Presenting that versified supplication, I placed his feet on my head and earnestly requested that he speak of his supremely holy life—outer, inner, and secret—without concealment or secrecy. However, because this lord maintained humility throughout his life while realizing the secret "just that," he said, "My life is without even a trace of meaning. There is no point in putting effort into deceiving others."

After many similar remarks, he sang:

"Listen, faithful son who desires liberation!
You have spent this life practicing the holy dharma
And view me, an old man, as your guru and a buddha;
You have uncontrived devotion.
There are many wondrous biographies and teachings of
All the past Kagyu siddhas and father vidyadharas;
They were very kind to their followers.

"Your life has not been lacking;
You've been blessed with the name of the Kagyu siddhas.[6]
Your deeds have not been lacking; your conduct is noble.
Your practice has not been lacking; throughout your life
You have been dharmically engaged in the benefit of
self and others.
You say, 'It is fitting for you to write your autobiography
To engender faith and devotion in us, your disciples.'
More than once, my intelligent son, Yudra Nyingpo,
And you, the kind Kagyu Tashi, have encouraged me
With pleasing gifts such as bundles of kusha grass
from Central Tibet
And feathers from poison-conquering peacocks.
As well, disciples from the south and the north have
encouraged me,
Saying, 'We really need your life story.'
But when I examine my being…

"The white snow lioness undisturbed by the
freezing blizzard
Had all her powers while in her mother's womb.

Once born, she surpasses all other animals.
This ability is inherited from her mother.

"From infancy, I have relied on gurus.
I have practiced their instructions.
But this body and mind are hard to tame.
Even now, I feel unsatisfied.
Because my knowledge of the view and meditation is not vast,
My life-story would not please holy beings;
Therefore there is no need to tell it.

"Although the golden-eyed fish adorns the Tsangpo,
    swimming through the water,
She is fearless because of the breath within her.

"I have associated with siddhas for a long time
And have concerned myself with developing the
    qualities of inner channels and winds.
Other than aspiration, my actual abilities are
    somewhat incomplete.
I have no qualities that would please those who have
    seen the supreme;
Therefore there is no need for my story to be told.

"The tigress of India with her vivid, smiling stripes
Roars with ferocity and blazes with wrath.
Although she terrifies small animals
She has few qualities beyond the stripes on her body.

"I am a humble old man
Who greatly enjoys relaxing and lying around like a corpse.

I consume delicious meat offered to me and do
    nothing in return.
I shamelessly enter the neutrality of sleep behind
    closed doors.
Such an old man has no life-story worth telling.

"Degenerate, I delay the morning.
My behavior is so bad that I am an outcast
    where I live.
I try to please laymen and women.
That's my story.

"In the sight of the holy
You need the excellent qualities of relinquishment
    and realization;
A fine writing style to please the learned;
And teaching, debate, and composition about
    traditional texts.

"To please most people you need to be like them,
To lie and sound good doing it.
I'm unskilled in such explanations,
So I lack a story worth telling.

"Because of my great years,
I've forgotten whatever I've done
And remember no stories worth telling.
So, please don't speak pointlessly."

After saying that, he wrote only his outer life-story; the inner and secret ones remained unwritten.[7]

When the noble guru was in his seventy-third year I went to his seat. Although considering my meager learning, intelligence, and so on, it would seem unfitting to inflict my nonsense verse on his ears, I submitted the following in the hope that it would interdependently cause the composition of at least a partial account of his true life:

NAMO GURU!
Father, buddha of the three times, protector of beings,
Smile with love and compassion.
Don't regard this request as trivial.
Please listen to me for a moment.

In the past, at the changeless vajra rock,
The abode of the glorious, great Guru Rinpoche,
I and my brother Yudra Nyingpo
Repeatedly requested that you compose an
  autobiography.
Recently, in the month of Gyal,
I remembered your deeds.
I couldn't stand it! I had to come here!
The distance is not really that great,
But I'm very weak.
I ignored the journey's hardship.
Now I ask that you tell me properly
Your holy story.

In the family of the white lioness,
Powers are completely present while still in the
  mother's womb.
Once born, she surpasses other animals.

She flings her turquoise mane, the sign of her greatness.
I think she is the most wondrous of animals.

From youth, you have followed the holy.
You have practiced the path of generation and
completion.
This is utterly unlike the behavior of ordinary people.
Isn't that the greatest life-story?

The white fish swims in the water.
Through the power of her breath, she is unharmed
by the water.
The sign of her greatness is her round, golden eye.
I think she is the most wondrous of those who live
in the water.

You have been held in the thought of siddhas.
By means of feeding apprehended and apprehender to Rahu[8]
Your discernment of things has blossomed from within.
Isn't that the wisdom of the siddhas?

The orange tigress so fearsome to see
Lives in the sandalwood forest
Roaring ferociously and eating human corpses.
She is resplendent with smiling stripes, the sign
of her greatness.
I think she is unlike ordinary predators.

You are the crown ornament of hidden yogins.
Appearing to live in accord with the world,
You have naturally traversed the stages and paths.

Your mind has reached the royal palace of the dharmakaya,
As was predicted by the Tathagatha.[9]
I understand these to be the deeds of an excellent
  bodhisattva.

Not trying to please those close to you,
But benefiting beings appropriately
With impartial love
Is obviously not the way other people behave.

You may displease thinkers with unworkable minds
And those more foolish than animals,
But, peerless lord who sees with twofold wisdom,
Many great beings abiding on the levels
Have repeatedly placed your lotus feet on their heads.

You turned my vicious mind to the dharma.
Your imprint on both tradition and realization is visible.
Even if you keep all of this secret, it will be uncovered
  in the future.
The thunder of your fame will resound through the sky.
The sunlight of your excellent deeds will spread all over.
The spectacle of your spontaneous, dual benefit
Will be seen by all, beyond this generation.

If such a life-story were presented clearly,
It would please future disciples of your lineage.
So, please let it be put in writing.

That was my request. In response, he said, "I've never, in this life, had a high social position or behaved like a holy person.

I therefore never intended to write an autobiography and have never kept records of what I did or thought. In fact, such a thing never occurred to me. So, I won't be able to describe events in detail or in the correct sequence. Because of my age, I won't be capable of fine words. However, in order to fulfill the hopes of you disciples, because I have offered many empowerments and transmissions to the victorious fathers and sons, and because some might feel they've made the mistake of relying upon an ordinary old man as the lord of their family, I will tell you a little. Write it down without adding or removing anything."

Then he sang this vajra song:

> "I bow to the glorious lord of the six families, Vajradhara,
> The protector, the lion of humanity.
>
> "My stubborn, intent son,
> Your request is stuck in my mind now!
> If this old man doesn't say a single word,
> You'll hear no answer to all you've said.
> Since even inanimate rock answers with echoes,
> Why wouldn't a human being endowed with the
> six elements?[10]
> Therefore, I'll tell you something.
>
> "I wouldn't boast in the company of others,
> But I can't turn away your faith.
> My deeds of body, speech, and mind
> Are best known to me.
> The stories I will tell you will include all I remember.

They are true and undistorted.
I will abandon exaggeration of good and bad.
There is no fault in the spontaneous recounting
Of my vague recollections.
Therefore I will tell my own story.

"My intelligent sons are more learned in fine words
    and composition,
But inappropriate exaggeration would be a shame.
An ordinary being requires no denigration.
Cast praise and disrespect to the winds!
You have been closely connected to me by good karma
For many lives in the past.
Write down this genuine life-story, whatever I remember,
As I tell it."

I faithfully placed the flower of his command upon my head, and wrote down the life-story, of which that was the first part, a description of the circumstances under which the autobiography was composed.

This sapphire, the wondrous essence of the sea;
This jeweled beacon that illuminates the hidden
    meaning;
This source of all accomplishment, the jewel of the
    nagas—
When it appeared as the ornament of the faith of the
    fortunate,
With satisfaction like that of attaining the first level,
I was delighted to write down this secret vajra speech.

Virtue in the Middle,
The Actual Autobiography

First, an Account of Previous Lives

I asked, "Who is the source of the venerable guru sambuddha's emanation? What were your previous lives?"

He replied, "It is extremely unlikely that I would be able to remember my source of emanation or previous lives; such things are not within the experience of ordinary people. However, if I say something about this in reliance upon the kindness of the second Buddha, Guru Rinpoche, and on that of the great treasure revealer, the king of dharma, Orgyen Chokgyur Lingpa, it would have to be asserted that my source of emanation is Manjushri, the lord of the ten stages, the embodiment of the inexhaustible, ornamental wheel that is the secret speech of all the three times' victors. The births emanated from him, both superior and ordinary, are beyond anyone's reckoning. However, to mention a few of the most significant ones:

"In the presence of our Teacher, I was the bodhisattva Marutse.[11] He started out as a common, unregenerate butcher. Our Teacher told him never to eat the flesh of a lion cub or marry the daughter of a king. Eventually two great kings, one of them Buddhist and one not, came to be at war. The Buddhist king enlisted the aid of the butcher and his gang, paying them well. On the way to battle, amidst the snows, they came across a lion cub, which his gang offered to the butcher as food. Remembering what our Teacher had said, he didn't eat it. Through the merit of that, when the opposing forces heard his name mentioned, they surrendered and became Buddhists. Delighted, the victorious king gave his daughter to the butcher as a wife. Again remembering what our Teacher had said, he was unable to accept her. Through the inconceivably great merit of that, he finally became a bodhisattva on the tenth level.

"After that, I was the great master Manjushrimitra of India. He went to Vajrasana and studied, becoming the crown ornament of the five hundred panditas. One day, in an assembly, he asked, 'Who has instructions that bring buddhahood in one life?'

"He was told that a seventeen-month journey's distance to the west, on Golden Ledge Rock Mountain, lived the teacher Pramodhavajra, who had been taught by Vajrasattva.[12] Having heard that, he went there and received introduction to the Great Perfection by means of symbol. In accordance with his guru's prediction, he meditated in the charnel ground of Hechendal in Sumatra, accomplishing the rainbow body of great transference.

"Later, I became the mahapandita Naropa, the learned guardian of Nalanda's north gate. That lord became supreme among all who taught the five sciences. When he attained common siddhi, his personal deity made a prediction. In accordance with that, he placed the feet of the nirmanakaya Tilopa on his head and underwent twelve great trials at the risk of his life. By doing so, he attained the supreme siddhi. He appointed the Tibetan Marpa as his regent and departed for the celestial realms without relinquishing his body.

"In this snowy land, in the presence of Guru Rinpoche, the second Buddha, I was the embodiment of the inexhaustible, ornamental wheel of his body, the lord of a thousand kila-wielding Tibetans, Nupchen Sangye Yeshe. When the great Guru Rinpoche gave the great Empowerment of the Eight Dispensations, *The Sugatas' Assembly,* to his pure retinue possessing karma, Nupchen's flower landed on Yamantaka. He was therefore especially given the tantras, agamas, and upadeshas of that deity.[13] He practiced at Draki Yangdzong and other places, and demonstrated various signs of siddhi, such as piercing rock with his kila and sitting on the sun and moon. Especially, through taking liberation as the path and collecting the life-force of the ten objects, he lived for six hundred years. Having attained the eleventh level, utter luminosity, he went to Changlochen[14] without relinquishing his body. His meditation teachings still exist, having come down through unbroken lineages of command and treasure.

"Later, I became Gyashangtrom Dorje Öbar, who held the treasury of the profound treasures of the Ancient Secret Mantra tradition. He retrieved from Yungdzalungmo treasures called *Manjushri, the Black Lord of Life; The Iron Scorpion; The Hundred Collar-Pouches of Nupchen;* and others. He held the dispensation of forceful mantra.

"He was reborn as Gyatön Tsöndrü Senge, who retrieved a Yamantaka cycle from the Boiling Tiger's Lair at Parotsal Red Rock.

"He was reborn as the treasure revealer Trime Kunga, one of the renowned Three Trimes. He retrieved many profound treasures from the Lion-Faced Rock below Samye Chimpu—*Gurusadhana, Great Perfection,* and *Great Compassion* teachings being foremost among them.

"In Kham I became Tsasum Terdak Lingpa, who retrieved many profound treasures from Samye Chimpu and the assembly hall at Shotö Tidro, *The Very Profound Padmaheruka* foremost among them.

"As for the Later Tradition of the Subsequent Translations, I was the noble Milarepa, the common ancestor of all siddhas in this snowy land. This lord first received forceful mantra from Nup Kulungpa and others, by means of which he annihilated all of his enemies. After that he appeared before Rongtön Lhaga, from whom he received the Great Perfection according to the Early Translations. After that, as had been predicted, he went to Drowolung in the south and bowed to the feet of Lord Marpa. He received the complete treasury of secrets, especially *The Three Gems of the Oral Lineage.* Immersing himself in practice at Lachi Gangra and other places, he attained siddhi. Of his heart-sons, the sun-like one was Dakpo Daö Shönnu and the moon-like one, Rechung Dorje Drakpa. Led by them, there appeared innumerable disciples who caused the doctrine of the lineage of accomplishment to flourish.

"I also became Lord Sönam Zangpo of Kyodrak Monastery, who held the lineage of the glorious Barompa Tarma Wangchuk. This lineage was one of the meditation communities that arose in eastern Tibet. The protector, Sönam Zangpo, relied upon Langre Drakpa Gyaltsen as the lord of his family and received the complete *Golden Dharmas of Barompa.* Immersing himself one-pointedly in practice at the Golden Cave of Chapti, at the Dakinis' Throne, and in other places, he became able to fly in the sky like a bird, to crush the hardest rock as though it were mud, to bring all that appeared to him under his power, and to overpower what appeared to others. The thunder of his fame resounded throughout China, Tibet, and Mongolia. He gathered all sorts of people together and established them in dharma. He had countless disciples, headed by the six dharma lords equal to him, such as Marmo Sönam Döndrup.

"I also became the great abbot Sönam Yeshe, one of the eight realized heart-sons of Mase Lodrö Rinchen, the lord of siddhas. This abbot engaged in boundless study of the sutras and tantras, and in practice of the essence. He perfected all the qualities of relinquishment and realization, and was appointed the regent of the precious mahasiddha. His rebirths—the life-long retreatant Sönam Gyamtso, Sönam Gyurme, Sungrap Gyamtso, Sungrap Trinle Rapgyay, and so on—were an unbroken stream of emanations of great service to the Surmang Kagyu doctrine through countless dharmic and mundane deeds.

They upheld the teachings of the Oral Lineage of Surmang and caused them to spread in all directions.

"As well, we can extrapolate from my having been Sangye Yeshe, which was recognized by the precious, great revealer of treasure.[15] Since that lord had mastery over karma and birth, my emanations must have included ordinary people, birds, beasts, bridges, boats, medicine, and everything else that is of direct or indirect benefit to one and all—a vast cloud of magical display. Although I'm usually unable to remember my past actions and lives, at times, through the blessing of my personal deities, in the experience of sleep combined with luminosity, when I have gone to places with which I was very familiar in the past, and when I have met certain individuals, various thoughts have arisen within me. However, I see no need to talk about that in detail."

That was the first part, an account of previous lives.

> Your nature is the space-like dharmakaya.
> Although perfectly awakened in the primordial
> expanse,
> Through the miracle of your excellent, profound
> intention
> You create inconceivably numerous clouds of oceans
> of emanations,
> Which moisten the soil of whoever is to be tamed
> And ripen the seedling of their awakening.

Virtue in the Middle,
The Actual Autobiography

Second, an Account of the Essence of This Life

I then received, over time, an account of the noble, precious guru's life, starting with his birth and ending with his eightieth year, which I wrote down as follows:

"As for a description of the arising of this life, this aggregate of the six elements arose in the following way:

"The essence of the speech of all victors, the teacher omniscient regarding the three times, the Lord Mahaguru, together with an inconceivably vast gathering of attained viras and dakinis,[16] such as the twenty-five disciples—that pure retinue which is the play of his five inexhaustible wheels of ornament[17]—is now living and teaching on the Copper-Colored Mountain in Chamaradvipa. With his compassionate gaze, he looks upon all beings throughout space and especially all the people of this snowy land with the love a mother bears for her children.

"The dance-like play of his activity is as agile and quick as lightning. He releases inconceivably numerous emanations and further emanations who, through the teachings of the profound treasures, heal the agitation of this time and establish beings in bliss. He is the sole protector of the people of Tibet.

"The way in which this body of mine arose like a magical illusion as the miraculous appearance of compassion for beings of the present time of degeneration, when the life-expectancy approaches twenty years, was as follows.

"Guru Rinpoche looked upon the place of my birth, Lei Darlung, in the southeast of this snowy land. With love he looked upon my retinue—the wild beings of the dregs of time, who are hard to tame, coarse, very afflicted, and have bad karma. From his heart issued a ray of white light, like that of the moon. This entered Nuptön Sangye Yeshe. From his heart issued a ray of light the color of vaidurya, and from Yeshe Tsogyal's heart emerged a sphere of light like blood. These two became mixed into one sphere.

"Then Guru Rinpoche looked upon my father—Rakshul Menlha Targyay, a rebirth of Takkar Apo, an exemplary man by either standard, of noble family[18]—and my mother, a rebirth of Mönmo Tashi Khyidren, descended from the family of Jangpön Dopal.[19] I was born to them.

"For the eight months of my stay in my mother's womb, I perceived it as a palace of crystal, and could see and know everything surrounding us. I could hear external sounds, and with some effort could ascertain their meaning, such as a discussion of the provisions and yaks my Uncle Chöpak was going to take on his journey to Central Tibet. All of this was somewhat dreamlike.

"Guru Rinpoche looked upon the time of my birth, in the evening of a 'fierce day,' during the waning phase of the twelfth month in the Male Fire Monkey Year, called Dongen, of the fourteenth cycle.[20] Although it was dark at the time of my birth, the light of my body, like that of the moon, illumined my surroundings.

"Two or three days after my birth my paternal grandfather, Tenpa Targyay, took me to Surmang on the back of a black horse that we had and presented me to the Refuge and Protector, Karmapa Tekchok Dorje. On the way back, I put on the red protection knot that he bestowed on me.

"At that time I understood conversations, such as my Uncle Tsangyang's account of his journey to Kawa Karpo, but couldn't yet speak. I would laugh when I remembered my previous, virtuous habits and I would cry when I remembered the bad ones. In my dreams and experiences I bound by samaya a demonic naga that lived down from our valley, and I subdued many male and female samaya-corruptors. I was vaguely aware, in a childish way, of many past, present, and future events; this gradually disappeared as I got older.

"When I was between four and five my mother went to receive guidance on the mind from Lama Nawa of Goche Monastery. I received it along with her and understood the instruction on how to foster stillness and occurrence. Thereafter, during the day when I went to the children's playground, I rested my mind a little. At night, when I went to sleep in my mother's lap, I discussed my doubts with her. In that way, I began to gain a little experience.

"When I was almost six I met Pawo Tsuklak Chögyal. I gave rise to the certain perception of him as Guru Rinpoche. Once I received the blessing of that holy one, previous good habits began to be awakened. I made the repeated aspiration to emulate him. At that time, his consort, the wisdom dakini Pumo, gave me a fire-starter and a ball of rock sugar. This established the interdependence for my taking bliss-emptiness as the path.

"One day, while I was near our home in Lei Darlung, I saw the eight emanated forms of Guru Rinpoche. One night, I dreamed that I met Guru Rinpoche in person. He bestowed the blessing of his three secrets, and told me that Lei Rock was equivalent to Mönka Rock in the south; that it had been a place for accomplishment assemblies; that it contained an imprint of his body; and many related things. Finally he said, 'Tomorrow, circumambulate the mountain and lake. This is important.'

"On the next day, because I was learning to read, I was not allowed to go out during the morning. Then it became very hot, and, without anyone noticing, I went, as though it were incidental to my play. I played in the water from the spring on the right of Guru Rinpoche's practice cave at Lei. While doing so I washed in it and drank from it. Within the swirling water of the spring, relics of the bodhichitta of Guru Rinpoche, father and mother, appeared suddenly. I dug a basin adjacent to the spring on the cave's left and diverted the water from that spring into it. The water brought me a thumb-sized image of Uddiyana Vajradhara, in sambhogakaya costume and in union, made from the bodhichitta of Guru Rinpoche, father and mother.[21] Well-formed, it appeared at a casual glance as though made from calcite.

"I was so delighted that I dared tell no one. I returned home and hid the image and relics in the rafters of our roof. Everyday I would take them out to look at and then hide them again. One day I went to my uncle's, where I studied reading, and saw the hide of a musk deer there. I asked him to cut a piece out of the neck and help me make a small pouch. I then put the statue and relics in the pouch and wore it constantly around my neck. I didn't tell anyone what was in it, not even the wind.

"One day in my seventh year I accompanied my uncle when he went to prepare goods for sale. Beside the Yilung spring I saw many beings with the upper body of a human and the lower body of a snake, yellow with black spots. The principal among them, who was bright yellow, stretched toward me, but I couldn't reach him. I asked my uncle to pick him up, but he paid me no attention. I continually saw Yögyal and the other spirits of our area; they were extremely protective of our family.

"My parents became anxious about the depredations of the many brigands in our region. I became angry and did various things to suppress the bandits, who subsequently disappeared without a trace.

"When I was in my tenth year an epidemic spread throughout all of Dokham. Either Tsogyal or Mandarava—I'm unsure which one it was—told me there was a treasure in a hut in front of Rele Dargyay Chödzong that would help alleviate the epidemic.[22] However, I was too afraid of my tutor to mention this, and so it disappeared.

"When I was enthroned at Surmang Namgyaltse, and staying there, whenever the invitation to the protectors was recited in the hall of protectors, I would perceive myself as the Four-Armed Protector and feel that it was time to go to that hall.[23]

"When I was in my eleventh year, I went to Palpung and met the Refuge Lord Tai Situ Padma Nyinje. I received the blessings of his three secrets and an extraordinary introduction to the ultimate meaning. From then on there was no change in my recognition of the nature; he transferred his wisdom to me.

"While at Palpung, I went to see the cotton dharma.[24] That night, I appeared to meet all of the gurus, starting with Vajradhara, of the lineage of definitive, ultimate realization. Afterward, in accordance with the divination of Nemdo Kulu, I entered retreat at Surmang Monastery in order to do the longevity practice from *The Embodiment of the Three Jewels.* While doing so, on the night of the tenth-day feast offering, I was awakened by a cracking sound without apparent cause, and by the sound of music. A beam of white light, like an unfurled bolt of silk, was shining on my pillow. Within the beam were many letters of treasure symbol-script, glowing like pearls. Examining them, I discovered the first list of my future dharma, wealth, and substance treasures. At the same time, I experienced the actual sight of Guru Rinpoche, father and mother.

"In my fourteenth year, while I was assisting in the painting of Namgyaltse, the Protector Maitreya Vajradhara, Tai Situ Rinpoche, passed away out of consideration for the benefit of beings in other realms. I made offerings one-pointedly. That night, I dreamed of Rinpoche, who appeared youthful, handsome, and radiant. He gave me much guidance about the correction and enhancement of realization, and repeated his previous exhortation to me to serve the teachings of Surmang.

"When I went on pilgrimage to Kyodrak, as there was the custom of drinking a mouthful of Guru Rinpoche's bodhichitta in the cave of Yumne Wakyung Draktsa, I went there to do so, and found a thumb-sized image of Green Tara made of jade. That night I dreamed that someone told me that it had been the practice support of Kawa Paltsek.

"That summer, while I was at Surmang, I dreamed that a man wearing white clothing said to me, 'Tomorrow, you will find a wondrous implement.'

"On the next day, I went with an old monk to fetch water. I found, amidst the rubble on the mountainside caused by the previous day's violent hailstorm, a hand-sized copper kila decorated with turquoise. I later offered it to the precious great revealer of treasure.

"When I visited Doti Lhatse, by the door to the cave there I found a wonderful, particularly well-made vajra of bell-metal.

"In my sixteenth year I went to the seat of Akanishtha Karma Monastery, where I met Dabzang Tulku Rinpoche. He gave me ripening instruction in the Six Dharmas of the Kamtsang tradition, on which I meditated one-pointedly. One morning, between sessions, I looked out of my window and saw, on the face of Mount Pomrak, the Lord Dabzang Rinpoche, the size of a small mountain, as brilliant as a hundred thousand suns. I received the four blessing-empowerments.

"When I practiced the empty enclosure, I saw my body as Vajrayogini's, and all appearances as bright red in color. I asked the guru about this, and he said that it was a sign of training. When I practiced the breathing, the stillness of mind's nature became very stable, without any distraction or bewilderment arising for many days and nights. My practice progressed, and I achieved the beginning of one-pointedness. At that time ice appeared beneath my seat, which the guru said was a sign of gaining control over the water wind. When I meditated on the great fire of chandali, I generated such heat that, although it was winter, no snow settled on the roof above my room. The ten signs described in the texts appeared to an acceptable degree.[25]

"When I practiced the other dharmas, the experience of what appears and what exists as illusory, and the ability to emanate within and transform dreams in various ways arose. Padma Tenkyong, in order to test the extent of my experience, threw many spear-like projectiles at my retreat house from all directions.[26]

"One night I dreamed that Datrul Rinpoche, wearing the costume of a heruka, appeared in the sky before me and taught me a wondrous technique for illusory body meditation. When I subsequently asked him about this in person, he said that there would be benefit in my meditating on and teaching it.

"When I was painting the murals at Namgyaltse, continuing the work I had begun earlier, I saw the five protector dakinis led by Chöpen Drinzangma several times in actuality, in meditation, and in dreams. They gave me their life-essence mantras. There also arose the appearance of my being assisted by the speedy messengers.[27]

"When I first attended *The Feast Dance of Surmang,* the appearances of this life were transformed and I felt that I had reached Akanishtha. Especially, during the invitation, innumerable wisdom, activity, and karmic viras and dakinis appeared, performing vajra dances. Above the mandala's canopy appeared Vajradhara and the other Kagyu forefathers.

"Datrul Rinpoche came to Surmang to bestow the novitiate and full monastic vows. My tutor told me to take them. I privately asked Rinpoche what I should do, given that I was of a passionate disposition and had the tendency to discover treasure.[28] He told me that most past siddhas had possessed the three vows,[29] and he explained in detail the distinctions among the three vows, how to keep them, and so on. He said that there would be no contradiction in my taking monastic vows at that time, and that he would 'see about the future.'

"As my sister, Dechen Chödrön, was the predicted treasure-consort of the precious great revealer of treasure, I presented her to him.

"On the day when Terchen Rinpoche retrieved the Kila chest of *The Seven Profound Cycles* from Karma Damchen Rock,[30] I served as activity vajra master. When I was carrying the tormas my way was blocked by the crowd. My experience blazed; with my left hand, I grabbed a young man by the scruff of his neck and tossed him far away, as though he were a feather. While performing a ganachakra, Terchen Rinpoche broke the treasure seal. Out of the place of concealment, hot sand trickled down. From the midst of that, he removed the kila-shaped chest, which, as all could see, was blazing with fire. I saw this.

"Terchen Rinpoche said, 'These are the qualities of Guru Rinpoche's wisdom mind's blessing. Don't all of you believe this?'

"Saying that and other things, he took the chest into his hands.

"I was immeasurably delighted. My mind became utterly clear, and I left a distinct footprint in a boulder that I walked on.

"Terchen Rinpoche told me at that time that I was, as a rebirth of Nupchen Sangye Yeshe, an inheritor of both *Tukdrup Barchay Kunsel* and the teachings on *Yamantaka the Lord of Life* from *The Seven Profound Cycles.*[31] He gave me the 'blood-drinker kila,' a practice kila of Nup's that he had retrieved from the sealed practice cave of Guru Rinpoche at Cham Nabundzong. Through the noble Terchen's blessing, I remembered a few of my previous lives, and was able to properly perceive his qualities. I felt the joy of a son reunited with his father; our minds became as one. I received all of the empowerments and transmissions of his new treasures.

"At Karma Yerpoche the tertön and his disciples convened a Great Accomplishment Assembly of Vajraheruka and Vajrakila. One day, in the rays of light reflected by the vajra and bell in front of Datrul Rinpoche, I saw the face of Vajraheruka. Other visions appeared to me as experiences and dreams. One night while asleep I saw a male spirit wearing a ragged hat and clothing remove a sphere of light, like a lamp flame, from the pillow of Tendzin Norbu, Datrul Rinpoche's bursar, who passed away soon after.

"When I was painting the murals at the newly built Dechentse Hall at Surmang, I became extremely drunk one night and rested the next morning. I knew that my painting assistant, Chokro Ajik, thought badly of me, so I painted a depiction of the noble Milarepa, as accurate a rendering of what was in my mind as a reflection in a mirror, in the time it takes to drink a cup of tea. This mural later became famous as having been miraculously painted by me.

"Around that time the five protector dakinis, led by Chöpen Drinzang, displayed their forms and graciously assisted me as speedy messengers, in actuality and experience. I depicted them in a mural as I saw them.

"I went to see Karma Tenkyong, the realized one of Korong, who predicted my discovery of treasure and my taking of consorts.

"When I performed a feast offering in the Dorje Chong Cave, I saw viras and dakinis doing vajra dances including the unlimited dance of bliss. The wisdom of bliss-emptiness arose so strongly that I couldn't bear to move my body. I also received predictions of the discovery of thought treasure and sky treasure.

"There were indications of the presence of a great deal of dharma, wealth, and material treasure concealed by chaplains of King Trisong within the image of Maitreya at Mokpu; and that it could be retrieved if the treasure guardians were given offerings. However, a few people whose minds were disturbed by samaya-corruptors prevented this, so I deferred the retrieval. It was also clear to me that dance costumes of Surmang had been concealed from the invading Mongolian army in Bo Mountain, but I left them there because of a landslide.

"I went to Derge as the Terchen's attendant. When we reached Golung Cave, I saw Guru Rinpoche and his two consorts in the sky.

"At the Changlochen Palace in Derge, the Terchen added his golden countenance to those of the two Manjushri Protectors, and a feast of dharma ensued.[32] I had the good fortune to take part in this, and perceived it as the actual presence of the great Guru Rinpoche in Tibet.

"On the night we went to Dzamnang Lotus Crystal Cave, I dreamed that a light blue dakini pointed to the right side of the door to Tsogyal's practice cave. On the next day we performed a feast offering. In the evening, accompanied by Ngawang Özer, the Terchen's nephew, I went to see the cave and remained there at ease. A bright red spark appeared on the rock of the doorway. From the rock I retrieved the bodhichitta of Guru Rinpoche, father and mother, which I later used to make the image of him called *Source of All Siddhi*. I also retrieved powdered gold and a scroll listing my future discoveries. That night I dreamed of a woman wearing white clothing who told me to make the image of Guru Rinpoche, which I subsequently did. I offered it to my brother, Kyodrak Tentrul. With the remaining material I made many images of Guru Rinpoche, of which I would give one to anyone who promised to recite a million Vajra Guru mantras.

"On the way to this place was a treasure chest, but it would have been difficult to remove.

"At Tsadra Rinchen Drak, together with Kongtrul Rinpoche, I received the ripening empowerments and liberating instructions of *Yamantaka the Lord of Life,* when that treasure was first revealed. On the next day, the Terchen told me he had dreamed that I brought three sharp swords out of a great mountain as treasure. Within the swords' handles was a dharma cycle concerning Yamantaka previously unknown on this earth. He said his dream indicated that I would certainly achieve the power of forceful mantra.

"At this time I recollected, during several experiences and while awake, the deeds of Nup and other lives.

"In accordance with the command of the Terchen, I performed the approach to and accomplishment of *Yamantaka the Lord of Life,* in a cell at Palpung. I wore a crown of corpse-hair and the garments of a preta; I anointed my face with human ashes and meditated one-pointedly. The dakinis were pleased, and I became what I am now. My mouth and eyes appeared triangular, so that I frightened even myself. Various signs of siddhi appeared. At that time cholera was spreading in that region; I dreamed that by performing a forceful reversal of the epidemic I saved the lives of many monastics and laymen and women.

"After my completion of the approach and accomplishment, the Terchen bestowed on me the solitary lineage empowerment of *The Three Wheels, the Profound Pith of Yamantaka.* During it, I experienced the pure appearance of my guru inseparable from the bhagavat, the glorious heruka, as vast as the sky, along with the other main deities. As he performed each stage of the empowerment, I experienced the corresponding blessings dissolving into the respective places in my body.

"Then the Terchen went to Yarlam Sengnam Rock, where he discovered another list of treasures and a guide to the twenty-five sacred places. While he was doing so, I saw, among the rainbow clouds above us, the vast realms and forms of the victors of the five families. Between them were many groups of viras and dakinis, performing vajra dances and singing songs of bliss. On the southeast side of the peak, among the rocks, was a steadily bubbling brook. Because of the formation of the stones, I saw it as the wondrous life-water that flows from the vase held by Amitayus.

"When we left, because of the amount we were carrying, the pack mules had to be driven across the swollen river, rather than rowed across in the boats with us. One of them, a white Chinese mule, began to be swept along by the current. I prayed one-pointedly to Arya Tara, and saw White Tara on the surface of the rocks across the river. The oarsman chased the mule with our boat, and it made it to the other side alive.

"On that night we camped at the foot of a mountain. The younger monks were frightened by the wailing of many ghosts. I performed a singed offering and the visualization for banishing obstructors, and the wailing stopped immediately.

"When we were welcomed by a mounted escort sent by Dzigar Monastery, I saw the dralas of Ling and the spirits of the locality welcome us at the same time.

"I saw the image of Guru Rinpoche kept at Padma Öpung, Dzigar Rinpoche's residence, and perceived it as Guru Rinpoche in person.

"When I went to Tazik in Chamdo, I saw a practice cave on top of a round hill of rock, and remembered living there when I was born as a geshe called Jangchup. I remembered this in great detail, down to what I wore. The Terchen's consort, my sister Dega, said she remembered being my patron at that time.

"When I went to Kusha Gyalwa Yungdrung, I saw it as the mandala of glorious Vajrasattva surrounded by the peaceful and wrathful victors.

"When we were in Dorshung Yangkyilkuk, signs of obstacles arose. Therefore on the next day I remained attentive and stayed close to the Terchen as we went on our way. His mount, a horse offered by the custodian of Dzadra, threw him, but I caught him in the air and so he was uninjured. At Sokrunang, an uncooperative ruffian approached the Terchen, joking threateningly. He was restrained by my brother Dorje Pagö, at which time I saw the Lord and Lady of the

Charnel Grounds appear amidst a whirlwind and bind him.

"When we went to Kere Gang, both the Terchen and I saw the seven wild tsens appear to welcome us.

"We returned to Karma Monastery where Surmang Tentrul Rinpoche bestowed an accomplishment empowerment of the Eight Dispensations. During it, I saw him, in pure appearance, as the actual presence of Great Splendor, the Supreme Heruka. Drubwang Tsoknyi Rinpoche came there and bestowed the Drukpa Kagyu tradition of the Six Dharmas and the oral lineage of the instructions of Trung Atsara. I exerted myself in the breathing and physical exercises. The avadhuti appeared. I became able to pull up and distribute the drops without difficulty. One night, my body appeared as the transparent form of the deity, and I saw, clearly and distinctly, the structure of the channels, winds, and drops. At times, the coming and going of my breath became unapparent and my penis was retracted into my body. Khenchen Dabzang Rinpoche was at Karma Monastery then and graciously bestowed instruction in 'the lower gate of great bliss,' as a spontaneous commentary on *The Hevajratantra.* He gave me progressive instruction and the permission to rely upon the body of another. In accordance with the command of both Terchen Rinpoche and Drupwang Tsoknyi, I took Zadröntso, a woman of good family, as my first consort, and practiced bliss-emptiness.

"On the night after performing *The Subduing of Yama* in connection with the death of Ripa Lachung, who had died in a landslide behind Karma Monastery, I dreamed that I subdued a spirit with the body of a bird and the head of a monkey.

"While the Terchen was at Karma, I received progressive instruction from him on *Tukdrup Barchay Kunsel.* I subsequently entered retreat. While there, the water in my vase remained unfrozen; my amrita appeared to boil; and I dreamed of acquiring representations of the body, speech, and mind of awakened beings and of going to pure realms.

"Especially, in addition to these general signs, one night, in a mixture of sleep and luminosity, I was led to the west by Terchen Rinpoche. It seemed we reached a high pass at the end of Jambudvipa where he pointed off into the far distance. At that moment, the appearances changed and we were passing over a vast, clear, blue sea containing many island continents of varying appearance. Finally, the sea became red. Rising out of its midst was an enormous, orange-red, heart-shaped mountain of rock. On it were innumerable inhabited areas. In the center of these was a tall palace made of precious materials, with a walkway, an ornamental roof, and innumerable other features. From the right and left of its golden ledges were hanging silk ribbons, at the ends of which were fringes in the form of the sun and moon. In its upper chamber were the victors of the five families in samboghakaya costume, surrounded by bodhisattvas of the ten levels. In the middle chamber was Guru Rinpoche, the Overpowerer of Appearance and Existence, wearing the nirmanakaya costume, the lotus crown, a robe, and a cloak, surrounded by the twenty-five disciples and innumerable other vidyadharas with rainbow bodies. In the lower chamber was Guru King of the Rakshasas, ruby-colored, wearing the costume of a king, surrounded by many male and female accomplished vidyadharas. Beneath them was the king of the rakshasas, with upswept orange hair, wearing a human skin, fresh intestines, and other terrifying garments, seated on a corpse as a throne, surrounded by many rakshasas and rakshasis, with the appearance of overseeing the activities of his subjects and judging their samaya.

"In the hall to the right of the central chambers was Guru Rinpoche in heruka costume, surrounded by many pure vidyadharas, enjoying a feast assembly and engaged in the dance of bliss-emptiness. In the hall to the left was Guru Rinpoche Vajrachanda, brilliant blue, unbearably fierce, and surrounded by wrathful emanations of various colors, gingkaras, and accomplished mantrins wearing black hats and cloaks.[33] They were manifestly liberating and offering many of those worthy of liberation. Between the halls were various trees, such as red and white sandalwood and agarwood, and bathing pools. The entire palace was surrounded by a jeweled fence. Surrounding that mountain of rock, at the ocean's shore, were terrifying rakshasa cities, with buildings made of brick, decorated with banners of skin and human heads both fresh and rotten. Above them, at the eastern gate of the fence, was a rainbow pathway like an unfurled bolt of silk.

"I walked along that pathway. In front of the gate was a boulder imprinted with Guru Rinpoche's footprints. Standing in front of it was a frightening rakshasa who said, 'If you pray to that support, you will reach the central realm without impediment.'

"I did as he said, and, walking to the left, reached the central hall. On the left of Guru Raksha Tötreng I saw the dakini, Blazing Blue Light, wearing red clothing, with many other dakinis behind her. I prostrated myself and prayed to them. Guru

Rinpoche placed his hand on my head, bestowed the blessings of his three secrets, and predicted some of my treasures. Along with that, he said, 'Your name is Palchen Traktung Gaway Yeshe Dechen Barway Dorje, "Great Splendor Blood-Drinker Joyous Wisdom Great Bliss Blazing Vajra." '

"In that way, he placed the crown of this name on my head.

"Then one of the dakinis three rows behind him took me by the hand and, holding my hand the whole way, brought me back to my room on a pathway of light.

"I recounted all of this to the Terchen. He indicated that it had meaning. 'Barway Dorje' became my name at that time.

"In accordance with the previous advice of our Khenchen Dabzang Rinpoche, I took as a long-term companion a young woman from Putsang. She bore the marks of a dakini, and received the name Kachö Wangmo, 'Celestial Lady,' when she was given the vow of refuge. I remained with her at the Terchen's side, practicing the approach to and accomplishment of the three roots in general, and especially the wisdom of the third empowerment. The realization of great bliss beyond elaboration arose. I gained the qualities of relinquishing the eighty things that are transcended on the path of seeing. My previous, slight mastery of the channels and winds was enhanced; I identified the wisdom of bliss-emptiness.

"When I was in Tsangrong, obtaining the wood for the construction of Karme Sangak Podrang, the Terchen's residence, I dreamed that I came upon a large, wooden house with a felt curtain hanging from the eaves. Within the curtained area was an old man, who said he was a retreatant, chanting the supplication, 'Lord, essence of the three refuges' from *The Karma Kagyu Six Dharmas.* He was the local spirit of Ralo, and had received instruction in the Six Dharmas from Lord Dusum Khyenpa, but I think it unlikely that he was able to traverse the path as would a human being.

"In the Water Dog Year a son was born to my companion.[34] Datrul Rinpoche came, performed the ablution, and bestowed the name Karma Trinlay Palzang. The Terchen declared him to be an incarnation of So Yeshe Wangchuk. Later, when Taklung Matrul Rinpoche came to Kham, he commanded me to found a family lineage, which I did.

"Around that time, I dreamed of the dakini Namkhai Naljor. She was a disciple of Tratsa Tsunma Yeshe Gyen, the consort of the mahasiddha Trungmase, and was an accomplished yogini, identical in nature to Atroma, the consort of Kyodrak Chöje. Namkhai Naljor actually went to the land of Uddiyana in the west, and received a profound oral lineage from Vajrayogini. At the end of her life, she was able to pass to the celestial realm without relinquishing her body.

"In a combination of experience and dream, I saw her wisdom body fly toward me from the western sky like a vulture, with a whooshing sound, and land in front of me. She appeared as a middle-aged human woman with her hair flowing down her back. Initially, she spoke extensively about mundane things, but then she bestowed the instructions that she herself had practiced, which were profound, extensive, and as precious as one's heart. Finally, she flew off to the east.

"I recounted this to Dabzang Rinpoche, who remarked that if, in the future, the opportunity to continue her lineage arose, it would be good to do so.

"At Lhateng Monastery there was a great stupa containing a hundred thousand tsatsas that had been erected during the time of the Great Encampment of the Karmapa. When I viewed it, I saw the form of Dharma Lord Rangjung Dorje above the stupa's vase.

"While performing a feast offering at Rechungpa's Cave, I saw the pure appearance of Bernakchen and his consort, filling all the eastern sky.

"The spirit of a tirthika liberated by Drogön Rechen still haunted the forest behind the cave, menacing the region.

"My lopön, Lama Sangngak, requested the empowerments and transmissions of the Great Perfection teaching, *The Heart-Drop of Vimalamitra,* from the Terchen. I received it in its fullest form at the same time. The faith and devotion of seeing my guru as indivisible from Vimalamitra arose within me. Through his blessing, the meaning of the words entered my being, to the point of certainty. From that time to this, I have never cast meditation aside, and I think that I am now at the level called 'mature awareness.'[35] As well, wherever I have gone in the north or south, in accordance with the Lord Terchen's command, I have disseminated this dharma.[36] Innumerable disciples have given rise to authentic experience, which is solely due to the kindness of my guru, Vajradhara, the Terchen.

"I returned to my residence. When I offered the empowerments and transmissions of the Great Perfection teaching *The Heart-Drop of Vimalamitra* to Lama Sangngak and others at Surmang Tashi Lhudrup Ling, the monk Drupwang asked me to sing a song about my dharma realization. In response, I sang:

"This is my long song, a description of the path by
 this wanderer who has never seen it.

"Listen, children connected to me in the past:
Since you have persistently asked me to,
This wandering beggar will sing
Of the Buddha's teachings in the sutras and tantras,
Of the guru's guidance and the stream of instruction,
And of my bit of experience—
Just a seed, a reminder, a beginning—
Emulating the songs of our forefathers
And in examination of my being.

"There are no words here meant to irritate anyone.
Turn your eyes toward this, forefathers!
This is the meaning of the tantras, commentaries,
 and the forefathers' teachings.
It might even help someone's practice!
Don't be competitive, my peers!
Understand my words.
You'll turn out more dharmic than me.
Don't fixate on my words, beginners;

Reflect on their meaning.
If you practice the essence of this,
It is certain that you will gradually discover the
path of dharma.

"From the beginning, rely on a guru who has good
experience and realization
And whose being has blessing.
Through that, experience will arise in you.

"The outer view and conduct of the shravakas and
pratyekas, briefly put:
A timid cat roars a tiger's roar.
The cat wouldn't fool the great, fanged tiger,
But he's quick and agile, he eats meat and has claws.
He can overpower small animals.
He can at least find his own food.

"The inner training of the mahayana:
When a dog barks trying to roar like a lion,
It doesn't sound too good to a lion.
But prudent people stay away.
The dog is able to guard the possessions of others.

"The great, secret path of mantra and its result roughly put:
An eagle can fly to the peak of the wish-fulfilling tree,
Although it is certainly not as fast as a garuda.
The ocean of the two obscurations is dried to its bed.
The crown jewel of the naga-king is gained.
Although the eagle is small, its wings are more
powerful than others.'

"Everyone, listen to my song!
Its meaning bears the lineage's blessing.

"The source of the pratimoksha is Rahula.
The sources of liberation through the bodhisattva
    methods are Nagarjuna and Asanga.
The source of the river of the supreme vajrayana
    is Vajradhara.
From the blessing of father Naropa and Maitripa come
The dharma of the path of means and Mahamudra,
    the path of liberation.
The family is unmistaken, the glorious Dakpo Kagyu.
These instructions come from that lineage.

"Although the discerning don't need it,
Those like me should hear this.
The supremely learned who've achieved tolerance
    for phenomena
And mere sophists—have a good laugh!
Children, make a song of it!
Youths, make a story of it!
Old men, make proverbs of it!
All men and women of this land, make an oral tradition of it!
All of you, make of it what you will!
If it displeases you, leave it alone!
All of the above is just rambling remarks.

"E MA! The crown ornament of all existence and tranquility,
In this and all lives,
Father whose kindness could never be repaid—
I bow to the feet of the lord of all families.

"You've seen what's wrong with samsara—
suffering and affliction—
And have given rise to sadness.
Through the merit of pure virtue,
You've seen the benefit of blissful liberation.
The arising of renunciation is certainly the first
blessing of the guru.

"So that these bodies, hard to get, may be useful,
You have asked that I sing about the essential meaning
Of the heaps of dharma, rolled into one,
And the instructions left by past siddhas.

"This humble, worthless beggar
Is as lazy as the village dog at home
But sought like gold elsewhere.
The three jewels led me out of the lower states.
My kind parents gave me this body, with freedom
and resources.
The quintessence of the environment's four elements
came together.
The mother-like lord guru
Lovingly nursed me with the inexhaustible treasury
of instructions.
I drank the breast-milk of the three vehicles.
I crawled at play in the fields of reading and the sciences.
I was put in the playpen of the outer shravaka and
pratyeka yanas.
I heard the old men's tales of the inner mahayana.
I acquired the clever thinking which determined the truth.
I decided, for my own good, to conquer the single enemy.

Looking at the conditions, the appearance of
    external objects,
I sharpened the sharp weapon of discernment.
I donned the armor of patience to prevent wounds.
I carried generosity as provisions to please others.
I wore saffron to fool everybody.
I summoned the desire for happiness as my companion.
I sent the fear of misery ahead as a spy.
I left the ruination of the eight consciousnesses behind.
I easily crossed the passes and valleys of dharma
    of the indicative meaning.
At the pass which separates superiors from the ordinary,
On the tower of the four noble truths, I hoisted the
    white silk flag of accomplishment
Through the power of past aspirations.
I found the testament of all the lord sugatas,
The final teaching of the supreme Shakyamuni,
The book of the factors of awakening
Written by the two noble chariots,
In which two-fold selflessness was clearly taught.
I realized I had deceived myself.
I couldn't defeat the enemy externally,
But once this inner enemy, self-fixation, was killed,
The clouds of the eight consciousnesses vanished.
The afflicted mind's darkness was dispelled from its midst.
Externally, the moon of love and compassion shone.
Inwardly, the sunlight of bodhichitta spread.
Once ignorance, the hideout of the thief, was discovered,
Self-fixation, the thief, was caught.
All of his loot—the spoils of fixating on outer and
    inner things as 'mine'—

Was recovered.
The fortress of the eight dharmas was pulled down
from its foundation.
The root of all enemies was conquered then.

"Then, I thought I should support my family, for
the good of others:
My father and uncles, the sources of inheritance;
My mother and aunts, who kindly cared for my body;
My spouse, to whom I was devoted;
My nephews and maternal uncles, my sources of counsel;
My paternal relatives and sisters, my supporters;
My brothers and friends, my companions in
happiness and misery;
And my neighbors, to whom I entrusted my concerns.
I supported them lovingly, fearing their misery.
I tried to please them, wanting their happiness. I tried
and tried.
I gave them all the wealth they wanted and they still
weren't satisfied.
I spoke gently to them and wasted my breath.
I looked lovingly upon them and they never smiled.
I put food in their mouths but their bellies were never filled.
I caressed them with gentle hands and their expression
made me shudder.
I loved them from my heart but their malevolence ran wild.
Forget about gratitude!
They became even harder of heart.
This is the complexion of our time; this is what's
wrong with samsara.
Our bosses are hard to please.

Our leaders exact a heavy tribute.
It is hard to take care of beggars and servants.
We are exhausted by the demands of our families.
We disappoint our mothers.
Our boon companions look askance at us.
All our neighbors bear us grudges.
If you have wealth, it trickles away; if you don't, you're poor.
If you have a retinue, they resent you; if you don't,
  you're stuck.
Those you help harm you in return.

"So I threw off the enslavement of my family.
I came to view them as neither friends nor enemies.
I saw the pointlessness of all I had done.
I became certain that my enemies had been my parents
  in many lives.
I decided that my best friends were my enemies in this life.
Really, friends and enemies are no more than dreams
  born of habit.
When you awake, you laugh.
It's all an illusion that fools the eye.
The attachment and aversion of fixating on it all as
  what it seems to be
Is like a deer trying to drink the apparent water
  of a mirage; how could he?
You bewilder yourself through preference and prejudice.

"This is what I have taken as the view, meditation,
  and conduct.
I barely make it into the ranks of mahayana practitioners
  of the paramitas.

However, my guru, Vajradhara, said I was definitely
born into the ranks
Of practitioners of the profound and secret.
He empowered me as a supreme vidyadhara.
He gradually bestowed the vase empowerments that
made me worthy of
Four-fold fearlessness, the three vehicles,
And from outer kriya up to the limits of the secret.
He named me a king and crowned me.
He placed the emblems of means and discernment in
my hands.
He gave me the amrita of the secret empowerment to drink.
He bestowed the qualified consort for the path of the
third empowerment as my queen.
He conferred the kingship of words beyond utterance.
He gave me the jewel, buddhahood in the palm of
one's hand.
He appointed the paths of generation and completion
as my ministers.
He gave me the protectors of samaya as my strong army.
Merit and wisdom became my elephant.
I ruled the kingdom of yogic discipline.
I established the land, the path of union and liberation,
in bliss.
I collected the taxes of undefiled virtue.
With the example of past siddhas in mind,
And craving the lord victors' qualities,
I threw the golden wheel, the path of liberation, into the sky.
I rode the path of means as my steed.
I passed the royal lineage of blessings on to my children.
I placed the golden amulet of instructions at my throat.

I placed the many-colored robe of secret words on
    my shoulders.
I gazed upward with the eyes of faith and devotion.
I carried the sun and moon of unity in my hands.
Without falling into the abyss of samsaric bewilderment,
I turned the wheel of equal taste as means.
Not stuck in the narrow passage of the shravakas
    and pratyekabuddhas,
I soared like a garuda in the sky of dharmata.
I achieved the gods' victory of buddhahood
    beyond bewilderment,
The ultimate state.
I simultaneously established all beings, my mothers,
Throughout billions of worlds, in bliss.
This is what I have understood and practiced
Through the kindness of the kind father guru.
I'm not proud.
This is what I've devoted myself to from the heart.
My words may seem boastful, but they convey the
    meaning of the texts.
This is unmistaken; it is the guru's instructions.
So, my children, please do this too.

"In that way, I sang songs to tell my story and provide instructions for the practice of others.

"That summer, I went to gather dairy products, camping as I traveled from place to place. On the night I stayed at the head of a valley in Dorje Zam, I dreamed of Yeshe Tsogyal, dressed as a Tibetan woman, so magnificent in appearance that one would never tire of gazing upon her, accompanied by many women. She walked a little away from the others, and, pointing her finger, said, 'That spring down there is a residence of Jokpo, the Brahmin king of the nagas. There is a white boulder there, shaped like a tortoise. When I concealed a profound cycle of dakini dharma there, I placed one of my hairs on top of that boulder. Not only is it still there, it has multiplied! There are two. This is a sign that it is time for that treasure to be retrieved. So, son, take it out of there!'

"After saying that, she, with her retinue, ascended ever higher into space, and disappeared.

"My attendant monk was very tough and adventurous. Therefore although the site she had indicated was very dangerous, on the next day I asked him to go there, feeling that I couldn't let this opportunity pass. He went, and I stayed at the edge of the valley. The upper rock at the site was shaped like a haunch of meat. When it was removed, there was revealed beneath it a hollow area filled with the bodhichitta of dakinis engaged in yogic discipline, like cinnabar powder. As soon as the hollow area was exposed, a fragrance more beautiful than any we had smelled before filled the area, amazing my attendant, who put what he had found in my hands. Amongst it were many white and black relic pills and the scrolls containing *The Dakini Dharma Cycle.* Through the kindness of Guru Rinpoche, father and mother, there was not even the slightest obstacle to, or difficulty in, its retrieval.

"Then, one night, while I was traveling in order to fulfill the wishes of some patrons, I dreamed that a monk told me that on the next day the heart of the bodhisattva Ever-Crying would reach my hands. On the next day, while I was going along the narrow ledge on the right side of the eastern prominence of the mountain at Surmang Khyungkar, a few small stones suddenly trickled down in front of me. Among them I found a heart, apparently composed of either quartz or bone. Its ventricles were filled with relics of various colors. Since the protector of that treasure was the dharmapala Red Tsiu, he both predicted my discovery of it and put it into my hands.

"Kongtrul Rinpoche, on the way to escort the Lord Refuge Padma Nyinje's rebirth, who had been born at Jangnatso, passed through Black Lake in Gyal. The Terchen went to meet him there. They received from each other various empowerments, such as that of the nine half-moons of Vajraheruka. At that time, I recollected their past births as the Prince and Vairochana, that Ladro Tulku had been a dark, corpulent monk who performed ceremonies on behalf of King Trisong, and the earlier and later births of others as well.

"While the Terchen went to Yegyal and other places, I practiced the Karma Kagyu *Chakrasamvara* and *Vajravarahi,* as well as those of the Oral Lineage of Surmang, at Sangngak Podrang. Various signs, particular to each practice, arose. I experienced definite independence.

"Gyalwang Tekchok Dorje and Terchen Rinpoche met at the village of Bumdzong. While they were there, I recollected the excellent deeds of Trungmase Rinpoche. I saw that supreme place, Bumdzong, as the mandala of *The Dakinis' Heart-Drop,* surrounded by many viras and dakinis, radiating wisdom light-rays of five colors, like the colorful and brilliant light of crystals and butter lamps. On the night that Gyalwang Rinpoche bestowed a Vajraheruka empowerment, I dreamed that a large man dressed as a king, with a large retinue, gave me a crystal tube containing a five-pronged vajra.

"After that, when the Terchen went to Derge, I accompanied him as an attendant. At Lhundrupteng, when the two Jamgöns and the Terchen first bestowed *Tukdrup Sampa Lhundrupma,* I had the great good fortune to be its first recipient.[37] Both before and after this, I received inconceivable amounts of teaching—on the common sciences, on texts, as guidance, and as practical instruction—from the two Jamgöns, whose kindness to me was peerless.

"In a tent of felt in a nomad camp at Yarlam Benchen, I saw Black Jambhala.

"The Terchen went to Meseng Sheldrak to find the guide to the sacred sites of Gyamgyi Dhoti. On the night that we camped at Gyanak Peme, the activity protector Atsara told me of the place's history and promised to ensure our safe passage through the Chudru Pass.

"When the Terchen reconsecrated the White Stupa of Ga, I saw a remarkable stupa concealed by Guru Rinpoche for the protection of the area in the rock on the banks of the Lap River.

"The Terchen found the guide at Rinchen Sheldrak. Seeing indications that he should go to Gatö Jowo, he went there. When we first saw that place from the pass at Pelungpuri Kalma, both of us, master and disciple, saw our Teacher, the perfect Buddha, the fourth guide of this aeon, surrounded by the sixteen elders.

"Because the way from Nyatso Purdzong was blocked, we couldn't enter the valley and had to stay where we were. Nevertheless, we offered feasts, smoke offerings, and ablution to the Jowo of Upper Ga from afar. That night, in a state combining sleep and luminosity, I dreamed that we were at a high pass above that valley. Terchen Rinpoche flew off like a bird. I flew after him. We passed over Tibet, Nepal, India, and other lands within Jambudvipa, and then crossed an ocean, passing over many islands. Finally, we came to Chamaradvipa, which was the color of copper. In its center was the Glorious Mountain, the realm of Lotus Light. Its outer shape was that of a dharmakaya stupa, and it contained within it innumerable palaces. In its upper chamber was the dharmakaya teacher, All-Holder, surrounded by dharmakayas such as Changeless Light. In its middle chamber was the sambhogakaya teacher, Lotus-In-Hand, surrounded by an ocean-like retinue of sambhogakayas. In its principal lower chamber was the nirmanakaya, Guru Rinpoche, surrounded by innumerable emanated vidyadharas. I saw all this and alighted there. I received blessings and empowerments, and then appeared to return to where I was sleeping.

"We then began our return journey. On the way, when the Terchen opened the gate to Gyamgyi Dhoti, I saw that mountain as a crystal stupa built on a golden ground. Its apex reached the formless realms. In its vase were innumerable victors, such as the sambhogakaya victors of the five families. The mountain actually has self-arisen images of the eight close sons; I saw them as the actual bodhisattvas.

"At Sokti Dilgen we were welcomed by the seven wild tsens, who were awesomely powerful in appearance.

"In accordance with the Terchen's instruction, I went to Akanishtha Karma Monastery. On the way, near Nyaktö Damang, five-colored light-rays, unbearably bright, were reflected into my eyes from a spring. I descended from my horse and went to look at the spring. A brown stone chest was floating on the water. I took it and offered it to the Terchen. It contained a sadhana of the wrathful Vaishravana Riding a Blue Horse.

"The Fourteenth Gyalwang Karmapa sponsored a Great Accomplishment Assembly of *The Ocean of Dharma: the Assembly of Dispensations,* led by the Terchen and attended by 113 lamas and about a thousand others. I thought I had never experienced anything so wonderful in my entire life. Given both the location, Karma Monastery, and the participants, I felt you could justifiably call the assembly 'The Glorious Copper-Colored Mountain.' That was the degree of my certainty and extraordinarily pure perception.

"It was at that time that my brother, Kyodrak Tentrul Rinpoche, accepted from me the image of Uddiyana Vajradhara, father and mother, that I had found at the spring in Lei.

"On his way back to Tsurphu, Tekchok Dorje stopped at the Mantra Hall of Surmang, where he bestowed, without using any text, the empowerment for a Guru Rinpoche Gurusadhana. I experienced the pure perception of him as Guru Rinpoche himself. On the next day, I invited him to my residence, and requested his permission to commit the practice to writing. He dictated it, calling it *The Accomplishment of All Victors,* and assured me I was the first person ever to receive it. He bestowed the ripening empowerment and liberating instructions complete as one.

Although he did not allow me to use treasure punctuation in transcribing the text, it is definitely a mind treasure. Its blessing enabled me to decode the treasures I subsequently discovered.[38]

"When I went to Galung, at Lachido, the seat of Dulmo Tashi Özer, I saw Tseringma and her four sisters. She predicted that I would open the gate to the Lion's Sky Fortress of Dzipu. About fifty of us performed a feast and a smoke offering and then started to circumambulate the place. Because I was very drunk, I slipped on the rocks outside the practice cave. I stuck my hand out to brace myself against the outside of the cave, and left an impression of my fingers and my mala in the rock, which everyone saw.

"The water of accomplishment that had previously flowed to the left of the cave's front had dried up. I wrote the letter NAM on the rock with my saliva and the accomplishment water subsequently started to flow again. On the day we were there, rainbow clouds gathered above the place and a rain of flowers fell. On the cave's right was a spring containing medicinal lime. In it, I saw for a moment a medicine goddess wearing a veil of white silk. I therefore think it would be good for physicians to take their lime from there.

"I wrote a guide to the place recording the things I had seen. Through the place's blessing, various experiences flourished in me. I recollected the lives of our forefathers such as Dulmo Tashi Özer. Moved, I expressed my experience in song:

> "NAMO GURU. Lord Vajradhara, essence of the three bodies,
> Father, root guru—I bow to you from my heart.

"In this place that resembles the changeless ground,
On the side of this mountain shaped like a horse's head,
On this ledge of rock, the Lion's Fortress,
Is someone whose behavior is that of a common,
long-haired mantrin,
Who is, to call me by a nice name, a vidyadhara,
A yogin, if you look at my experiences,
A beggar who wanders aimlessly.
I will sing of external images
And of the inner nature.
I want, in my heart, to present offerings to the Kagyu fathers.

"At first, I thought of the ocean of samsara.
Using the image of a boat to represent freedom
and resources,
I dared to embark on a search for the jewels
of meaning.

"Second, I used the image of an illusory flower
To represent these changing aggregates.
I resolved that I was soon to die.

"Third, I used the image of my hope for happiness
and fear of suffering
To represent the causality of virtue and wrongs.
I chose what to relinquish and what to undertake.

"Fourth, I used the image of work that will never end
To represent the subduing of enemies and the protection
of friends.
I became utterly disgusted and nauseated.

"I took the ground, dharmata, as the direct cause.
I took examining it as the indirect cause.
Because I've seen it directly, am I ever happy!

"In its unlimited radiance, the appearances of samsara
and nirvana,
I saw no three aspects—just appearance.[39]
Is it ever luminous in the expanse of its nature!

"Although this display of variety never stays put,
We stray into samsara by fixating on it as real.
But when I searched for what things arise from and
dissolve into,
I ended up in the resolution of their emptiness.
The villainy of the thief—ignorance—was exposed.
The disastrous chain of mental formation broke by itself.
The rainbow of self-fixation vanished in the sky.

"There was nothing in this ground that could be
pointed out.
My path was to be free from the alteration,
Exaggeration, and denigration of whatever arises.
The sky beyond intellect was cloudless.
I basked in the sun, awareness beyond elaboration.
I took the moon, the experience of lucidity-emptiness,
as a companion.
The planets of bliss-emptiness appeared in the
background.
The stars of appearance-emptiness were innumerable.
Non-referential compassion for beings, the unity of
awareness-emptiness, was unceasing.

The forces of causality—adventitious, nonexistent
appearances—
Were overwhelmed by the attack of beyond-the-limits-
of-thought.
The royal palace of no-fixation was impressive,
But, as the person who gained it had no name,
Craving for its attainment was used up.
Because I saw that the attainment of the result is
a mere conventional isolate,[40]
I was without any fear of falling back into samsara.
I saw the river of hope and fear dry up.

"Now how happy is the meditating yogin!
This song of whatever experiences have arisen,
Sung in this place of blessing, this dwelling of practice,
Is offered to the holy tulku and his nephew,
To the faithful Anye Kuru and others,
To all who have provided resources,
To humans and non-humans alike,
As an inexhaustible feast.
May you all play the music of delight.
This is unlikely to be an expression of realization,
But since the descent of blessings is uninterrupted,
I do carry the implementation of experience in my heart.
I dedicate meritorious virtue to beings.

"That is what I sang.

"When I subsequently went to Nangtse Ritrö, I became convinced that it was the palace of the Great Compassionate One, Avalokita. One night I dreamed that when Guru Rinpoche was there an emanation of Paltreng, the goddess of medicine, offered him three pieces of arura, which he blessed and left there as the essence of the place. One day, while I was circumambulating, I sat down to rest on the site's left. Brilliant rays of white light, seemingly emerging from the clouds, and containing various letters such as TRAAM and TRAM, appeared to dissolve into the rock. When I examined the rock, I found many clear, large, white, self-arisen letters in the rock that had not been there previously.

"I stayed for a long time at the Samdrup Temple in Tridu. While there I relied upon Tsering Yangdzom, a young woman with excellent external and internal marks who had unfabricated faith and devotion, as a companion. When I was finally about to leave and return to my region of residence, she, loving me so much that she couldn't bear our separation, asked me to leave her with instructions that could serve instead of my presence. In response, this is what I sang:

> "Listen, young woman of family,
> Faithful friend of my heart!
> You have asked me, the yogin who wanders
> throughout the land,
> To sing you a memento of our love,
> Words to be kept in the heart,
> Instructions to bring your mind to the dharma,
> A song to ease your heart.
> Maiden, I will sing and sing!
>
> "Among worldly people,
> Fathers leave their sons advice,

Which few sons follow.
Worldly endeavors are meaningless.
Meditate on these instructions as advice for the future.
A stalwart son is his father's true son.
In the same way, if you can follow my advice, you
 will never be separate from me.
This is like a son taking after his father.

"Mothers talk kindly to their daughters.
Few daughters listen.
Worldly talk is meaningless.
Make devotion your conversation.
Daughter of a loving mother,
If you have faith, you will never be separate from me.
This is like a daughter taking after her mother.

"Masters instruct their servants.
Few servants do what they're told.
Worldly instructions are useless.
Meditate without respite on these, the essence of
 instructions.
If you practice dharma quickly, you are like the best
 of servants.
If you remember this, it is like a servant inseparable
 from her lord.

"This wandering yogin loves faithful men and women.
He sings songs of profound dharmic instruction.
Few keep his words in mind.
There is no need for songs as entertainment.
The point of my songs is attention to causality.

Disciples, keep that in mind.
If you can pray with a devoted mind,
The father guru's compassion is without 'near and far.'
This is you taking after me.

"The point of my words is this:
Think not only of this life, but of the next and beyond.
Reckon the results of right and wrong.
On the road that leads to either samsara or nirvana,
Don't choose wrongly between happiness and suffering.
Don't drown in the river of birth and death
Which feeds the ocean of samsara.
Get into the boat of practice!
Look toward the shore with eyes focused on liberation.
Bite your lip with the canines of fortitude.
With the strokes of generation and completion,
Holding fast to the oars of cause and result,
Row past the waters of distraction
To the island of liberation.
With faith and devotion, never forget
The kindness of the holy guru, your refuge and guide.
Girl who is fixed in my mind,
This is my response to your kindness.

"Sometimes, when you are practicing,
You will remember your friend,
This wandering long-haired yogin.
Let this little song, sung to dispel sadness, be my substitute.
Let it be the support for your faith and a source
of devotion.
Let my final words before I go

Be instructions that bring dharma to the path.
Let them serve as an aspiration to meet you often
And as a portent of our meeting soon.

"That was what I sang. She had found the three pills arisen from the blessing of the medicine goddess on the circumambulation path at Nangtse and gave them to me, at which time a spirit of the locality displayed his form, riding an elephant, and exhibited pleasure at our acquisition of these.

"After I left, she made good use of her freedom and resources by going into retreat for three years in the Cave of the Yetis. When she performed a hundred Severance feasts, she perceived the whole mountain collapsing and so on; she experienced inconceivable signs of the overcoming of upheaval.[41]

"After I had performed another approach to Yamantaka, I performed the reversal practice of the Kimkams called *The Mountain of Poison* for the benefit of the Surmang lineage as Terchen Rinpoche had directed me.[42] The tormas were carried off by a whirlwind, and a thunder and hailstorm suddenly arose. That night I dreamed that many men in armor told me they had killed twelve certain enemies of the doctrine. On the night I applied the same practice to spirits that were menacing the whole region, controlling them by means of Yamantaka, I perceived the three mountains of the district as three ferocious, man-eating tortoises with poisonous moles on their bodies and hair made of weapons. I stood up and, with the sun and moon in my hands, held them down so that they could not move. The guardian of Maseng Rinchen Sheldrak appeared at my window every night as an elderly man wearing a fox-fur hat to predict who was going to come there the next day and other things, and to provide various resources. I taught him much dharma of the indicative meaning. Since he also sometimes visits the Yunam Kokrong Cave, it seems that he is the guardian of these three places.

"After that, I took emptiness with the nature of compassion as my actual practice and recited as many of the six syllables as I could.[43] I began to experience imperviousness to circumstances. At this time, in the Water Rat Year, my companion gave birth to a boy.[44] The Terchen gave him the name Padma Tsewang Dechen Chokdrup Gyalpo, 'Lotus Life-Mastery Great Bliss Supreme Accomplishment King,' and pronounced him an emanation of Gyalse Lharje. When Taklung Matrul Rinpoche came to Kham, he recognized him as a reincarnation of the Madman of Bhutan, and told me that, as my son was a tulku of Taklung, he should live at that seat. However, I presented my excuses. Whether you consider the qualities with which my son was born or those he developed through training, it is evident that the Lord Refuge was unmistaken in his recognition. Most of the facilities for the practice of my teachings were established by this son.

"Having completed three years of practice, Terchen Rinpoche emerged from retreat. He asked me to come to his newly established Neten Monastery. I went there and served him in various ways, such as by making statues of the sixteen elders. One summer, in between such duties, I practiced the accomplishment of Vajraheruka, as well as meditation both with and without characteristics. While in the company of my companion, an extraordinary wisdom of bliss-emptiness was born in me. When the monks, led by Karma Monastery's Great Abbot, performed the rainy season retreat, I dreamed, on the night of the full moon, that I heard the sound of the clacker summoning the sixteen elders to the renewal and purification ceremony. One night I dreamed that the noble elder Naklane appeared at my door. He was youthful, pleasing, handsome, and tall. I invited him in, offered him food, and asked him where he usually lived. He replied that he lived at the top of one of the faces of Mount Meru.

"When I went to Ga, I gave Sönam Rinchen, the son of a local ruler, extensive instruction on the channels and winds, and on generation and completion. He practiced in extreme secrecy and various signs of attainment arose. Whenever a problem arose in his practice, I appeared to him either in a dream or in a vision and provided whatever guidance was necessary; his mind was at ease.

"When I attended the first performance of the Longevity Dance at Thrangu Monastery, the peaceful and wrathful deities of longevity appeared to me, actually performing the dance themselves.

"When I attended the Tenth-Day Dance at Benchen Monastery, I realized that the Dance Master, Karma Dargyay, was the rebirth of a mantradharin disciple of Nyangben Tingdzin Zangpo.

"While I continued to travel through Ga, I offered various instructions to Lama Jampal Gyaltsen of Nangtse, as I had in the past, and was also able to fulfill the wishes of Lama Kunga Chökyi Wangpo Rinpoche, who, having been connected to me in many previous lives, wanted detailed instruction concerning the essential points of generation and completion. His brother, Kunga Samten, a monastic, initially displayed disapproval of my lifestyle, but subsequently became especially devoted to me. I offered him a variety of instructions on generation and completion, and he is still upholding the banner of accomplishment at the Palgyi Ritrö Retreat.

"Because there was the suspicion that the spring to the left of the Vairochana of Bi bore two curses affecting the Traleg Rinpoches, I performed the *Destruction of Curses* ritual of *Manjushri Yamantaka the Lord of Life.* That night, I dreamed that a pandita told me that one curse was too old to uproot, but that the other had been pacified.

"When Terchen Rinpoche was encamped at Kyijam Sun Moon Cave on his way to central Tibet, I had vague recollections of some of the previous lives of many of the holy beings present there. I also saw on several occasions the guardian of that place, a great upasaka, in the form of a sixty-foot fish with eyes burning brighter than the sun's rays, his body covered with resplendent armor-like scales.

"On the night we reached Dilyak, I saw Datrul Rinpoche, appearing as the Four-Armed Avalokita, on the distant peak of an extremely high mountain of white rock to the east. Many people appeared to be assembled there, some of whom were saying that it was Avalokita and some of whom were saying that it was Datrul Rinpoche in their midst. I realized that they are of the same nature. Although at the time I couldn't actually see the mountain of Yamphu Rinchen Pungpa, because I saw the

Great King Vaishravana in its direction, I think that mountain is a residence of that god of wealth.

"While relieving myself at the foot of the mountain of Drepo Gyal, a great deal of earth and stone suddenly slid down the mountainside behind me. Among the rubble I found a chest of stone shaped like a tortoise. When I opened it, I discovered within it fifty-five crystal flowers of various colors, marked with symbol script. That night, I offered them to the Terchen, who said that they were a list of the profound treasures that were mine to discover. He kept a few of the flowers.

"When we reached Momo Tsadra, indications that it is a place of the three roots in general and especially of the Great Wisdom Garuda appeared.

"On the night we camped at Kawa Hril, we saw some bandits. We exhorted the protectors and chanted *The Pride of Nupchen.*[45] The seven wild tsens appeared ready to set upon those who threatened us, so the bandits were unable to harm us. Some of them were eaten by wolves. Later, others among them reported that they had seen the Terchen's tent and tent-poles blaze with fire and had thus been unable to approach.

"Terchen Rinpoche proclaimed the five hills of Bachok to be residences of Tseringma and her four sisters. I also saw this.

"When we camped at Nakchu Urgu, I heard wolves howling more ferociously than I had ever heard before. Among us was a young Chinese boy, said to be a rebirth of King Nyatri Tsenpo. He died there.

"Garwang Rinpoche and Tendzin Rinpoche, lacking provisions for travel, had to camp with us. They then went on ahead of Terchen Rinpoche's party.

"One day, while we were in the valley of Drunak, I looked in the direction of Sky Lake. I saw a very tall, blue dakini. I don't know who she was.

"At Damyangra Korchen, in the early morning, I saw a full moon that filled a third of the sky. My mind became brilliantly clear, and I understood that all phenomena are of the nature of luminosity.

"Resenting the Terchen's and my presence in that area, the spirit Nyingdrung Tsenpo possessed someone, who began to say various crazy things. I compelled him by samaya, and he peaceably left the person.

"When we were at the base of the border-taming stupa erected by the dharma King Songtsen Gampo, I perceived the whole area as the realm of the Thirty-Three Devas.

"The spirits of Tsaritra appeared to welcome us, and promised to provide for our needs on subsequent visits.

"Although the great nyen Thanglha was, in the past, very firm in samaya, he had lately become resistant to employment. Terchen Rinpoche accoladed him and reminded him of his samaya, as did I. Thanglha appeared pleased and did what we asked of him.

"At the hot spring where the naga king Dawa Lakyang resided, I saw him as golden with a snake's hood.

"Terchen Rinpoche entrusted activity, through the invocation of samaya, to the earth goddess Jomo Gangkar. When I arrived there, in the midst of a blizzard, I saw her in the form of a woman riding a deer. I compelled her with samadhi and reiterated her samaya.

"In the temple of Vajrasadhu below Yangpachen, I saw him.

"At the entrance to the valley of Tsurphu, the spirit Dridzi Lakser exhibited delight at my presence. At Akanishtha Tsurphu I rejoined the Terchen's camp. I saw the preserved form of the Lord Refuge Tekchok Dorje, who had departed for other realms, and met Drukchen Rinpoche, who was there at that time. I engaged in as much merit-accumulation and offering as I could. In the service of all the Kagyu, and especially of the Tsurphu Ladrang, I performed the protection and reversal rituals of Yamantaka. Signs of benefit appeared. I also performed a controlling ritual at the door of the Protector Hall there, at which time the vital force and spirits of many malevolent beings were visibly summoned in the form of pigeons.

"Because the previous Garwang Rinpoche had passed away at Nenang Monastery, there was concern about negative interdependence. I asked Drukchen Rinpoche what to do about this. He said that the full practice of *The Subduing of Interdependence* was needed. I therefore did this at Nenang, on Garwang Rinpoche's behalf, for twenty days. It became clear to me that, although the adversity affecting Garwang Rinpoche was successfully reversed, there remained a significant danger to Surmang Tendzin Rinpoche. There was no one with whom

I could send a warning, however, and so he passed away when he subsequently came there, which disappointed me greatly.

"I went to Lhasa and saw the Jowo and Shakyamuni images of the Buddha with the pure perception of them as the perfect Buddha himself.

"In the upper chamber of the Potala I saw the images of King Songtsen Gampo, his ministers, and his queens as the actual presence of those beings. While in the vicinity I saw quite a few sorceresses, some with form and some without.

"I performed the practice of Severance for the benefit of the local ruler of Namri Gopa. The local spirit appeared in the form of a large dwarf, saying, 'Forceful visualizations and compulsion will not be necessary. I will free him from his illness now!'

"The spirit seemed pleased.

"The Terchen arrived in Lhasa, and we attended the Great Prayer Festival together.

"Then my companion and I went to the Cave of the Moon in Yerpa. While we were there, a demonic spirit with a monkey's head and the talons of a bird landed with a whoosh on the peak of the mountain. I entered the samadhi of the Great Red Garuda and liberated the spirit. Thereafter that practice place proved very beneficial.

"In Yamalung I found an image of Guru Rinpoche made of naga clay, and in the river there, a jewel.

"At the Phakmodru seat I received the entrustment seal for a volume of teachings on the magical illusion of the dakinis, but lost it due to the negativity of some of those present.

"When I saw the representation of Machik Lapdrön at Zangri Karmar, I perceived it as Machik herself. My devotion blazed; I cried and got goose bumps. I then saw Machik dancing in sambhogakaya form.

"One day, while I was in Tsithang to see the sights there, I encountered fifteen women carrying water pots, walking in a line. The first of them had a counter-clockwise joy-swirl on her forehead, drawn with sindhura. Her lower lip bore the imprint of her upper teeth, and she was walking toward me in a hurry. She laughed and gazed at me out of the corners of her eyes. I knew that if I embraced her, Vajrayogini would lead me to the celestial realm that very day. However, out of concern for the teachings and for beings, I didn't do it.

"At a crossroads in that town, I met a yogin with a topknot, the mere sight of whom inspired faith in me. We conversed for a while, and our minds became as one. I looked everywhere for him the next day, but such a person was unknown there. I wondered if he were not an emanation of Guru Rinpoche.

"When I went to Yambulagang I saw the images of the king and his ministers as those beings themselves. As signs of blessing, rainbow clouds gathered, a rain of flowers fell, and light shone from the plateau. As I saw all the treasures concealed in the mountains there by the kings of the past, it is evident that they remain there undamaged.

"In the Cave of Rechungpa, I saw Rechung Dorje Drakpa, wearing the costume of a heruka, surrounded by the gurus of the oral lineage, and received instruction and blessings.

"When I saw the image of Vairochana in the Jatsal Temple, I saw the wisdom body of that deity.

"Then, when I was crossing the sandy plains on the way back, near Tsangrong, a cloud as white as a conch shell appeared in the midst of a perfectly clear sky. Within the cloud, I saw the form of Thangtong Gyalpo, the size of a mountain. It remained visible for some time.

"At Rakshasa Mountain in Palchen Chuwori, I recollected the vision of Chakrasamvara that the precious mahasiddha Trungmase had there. I prayed repeatedly and briefly saw Chakrasamvara with a body like pure gold.

"Then I went on pilgrimage to Tsari. On the way, at Yartödrak, I saw the spirit Yarlha Shampo, who seemed pleased. When I passed through Olka, the resident spirit Ode Gongyal demonstrated his pleasure by sending down a rain of flowers and bringing bright sunshine.

"When I was staying at Chökor Gyen in Dakpo, I heard a lot of versified predictions of future events in the sound of the river to my left, which I wrote down. These were taken, and eventually lost, by Dode, a cantor in the service of the Terchen.

"When I went to the Spirit Lake of the Queen of War, I saw within the lake a great blue palace surrounded by lots of trees, and also a blue mule running about within a black wind that swirled up from the lake's depths.

"At the Prostration Ridge on the way to Daklha Gampo, I prayed one-pointedly to the peerless Gampopa and his disciples. As I walked up the mountain, I smelled a delicious scent previously unknown to me, and saw, in the sky in front of me, the peerless Gampopa. He was like a mountain of gold—huge and golden in color—and wearing the three robes of dharma and the meditation hat. His right hand made the gesture of teaching and his left, holding a jewel, the gesture of meditation. He was smiling, and his presence was unbearably majestic. Surrounding him was a sangha of many saffron-robed monastics and others dressed as yogins, all of them standing. The moment I saw them, I threw myself to the ground in veneration and prayed.

"Gampopa said to me,

'E MA! All things without exception
Are non-dual clarity and emptiness.
Natural, spontaneous wisdom
Has the same taste as your mind.'

"When I heard that, a new cognitive experience of the naked, inexpressible nature arose within me, and I was left for a moment without thought. The body of the guru disappeared.

"Since Terchen Rinpoche had gone to Sangngak Chöling, I also went there.[46] I offered the Drukchen the treasure I had found below Drepo Gyal and a fine white turquoise found by my companion on the mountain behind Surmang. I had received indications that the turquoise was one offered to Guru Rinpoche by the Bhutanese woman Tashi Khyidren. Drukchen Rinpoche was delighted.

"Then the Terchen and his disciples, including me, went on our way as a traveling camp. We performed a feast offering at the Temple of Varahi. At first, because I was a sculptor, my mind became engaged in criticism of the statues in the temple. However, when we reached the actual feast itself, my perception was utterly transformed. The statue of Vajravarahi became the deity herself; the place became the realm of Uddiyana. No thought of ordinary appearances arose.

"When we reached a village of peaceful Lopas, the pure perception of all the men and women of its seven households as the sixty-four male and female deities of the Chakrasamvara mandala arose. We then traveled through the forest and encountered a few aggressive Lopas, who were intimidating. Through the activity of the dharma protectors, a lot of Bhutanese men appeared suddenly, which frightened off the Lopas, who fled into the forest.[47]

"When we reached White Lake, Terchen Rinpoche, I, and all the disciples saw, on the peak of a mountain like clear crystal, a blue source of dharmas framed by rainbow light. I saw, within the lake, the vivid mandala of the dakinis of mother tantra, the four vajra goddesses, with animal heads and various protector dakinis.

"In the sky above the Lake of Ekajati, amidst clouds, I saw the Great Matrika. She had one eye, one breast, and one leg, was purple in color, and held a knife and a skull.

"When we performed a feast at Lawa Cave, I saw a lot of cotton-clad yogins welcoming us, and a lot of deva and naga children consuming the dakinis' first offering.

"In the Valley of Human Skin, I saw a huge human skin stretched out above the valley, but I didn't know what that meant.

"At Pure Glorious Mountain, a great stream was flowing from the top of the mountain, which I took to be an indication that attainment would be unceasing.

"At Shingkyong Pass I saw the male and female Shingkyong, and at Podrang Chongmo, their male and female attendants.

"At the Feast Vessel of Dakinis I saw, for a long time, a lot of women dancing.

"When we reached Yeme, in the place of the eight nagas, I received as a blessing a few drops scattered from the ganachakra of many dakinis. There were two place-born dakinis there; I formed a connection with them.[48]

"As we traveled through Protector Rock, I saw Mahakala, with a body of light. While in that place, I perceived it as the realm of Heruka. Thoughts of ordinary appearances never arose.

"When we got back to Samye, I saw that there were treasures in both the Red and Black Stupas, but never got around to doing anything about them. While doing prostrations and circumambulation in the Aryapalo Temple, I saw sparks continually shooting out from the right side of the statue of Avalokita.

It was obvious that there was a treasure there, but I left it alone. In the Bodhichitta Temple, Terchen Rinpoche gave both the bodhisattva vow and an explanation of *The Bodhicharyavatara.* To this, Nedong Drupchen brought a large jar of liquor, which he concealed under his shawl. A few of us shared this among ourselves. Our experience blazed, and we danced and joked as people will when drunk. Nedong Drupchen asked me to demonstrate signs of attainment. I did so, in the following way, for the sake of auspiciousness:

"The Terchen's consort, my sister Dega, spent that whole day circumambulating Samye. She saw me accompany her the whole time. Everyone who attended the Terchen's teaching saw me stay there for the entire day. Others, walking between the temples of Samye, saw me accompany them. When, on the next day, we went to Zurkhar, one member of our encampment reported seeing me circumambulating the Stupa of Zurkhar, having already got there before everyone else. Another saw me at the front of the traveling camp, yet another in the middle of it, and still another at the rear.

"What we call 'miracles' happen under those types of circumstances and because of the attitude of the perceivers.

"At Samye Chimpu, Terchen Rinpoche bestowed the empowerment of the Great Perfection, *Lama Yangtik.* I saw the mandala as indivisible appearance-emptiness, and gained certainty in the indivisibility of the expanse and awareness. I practiced the separation of samsara and nirvana there for two weeks, during which time all pure and impure appearances arose in my experience and I mastered them. I saw, seated on and in front of the many boulders to my right, to my left, above, and below me, many panditas, siddhas, and translators. I remembered discovering treasure when I was born as Gyatön in Dzalhumo. I saw some minor treasures there but left them because of their relative unimportance.

"One day, when I looked down at Samye from Geu Dramar, I remembered the deeds of the father and son dharma kings, the queens, the ministers, and the subjects. I vaguely recollected the lives of most of the panditas and siddhas of that past time. This saddened me and I came to tears more than once.

"In Yamalung the Terchen, I, and all the disciples practiced the *Red Amitayus* from the New Treasures for seven days. During this, signs such as the boiling of the life-water and of the liquor in the kapala arose. In particular, I dreamed that wisdom dakinis holding life-vases bestowed deathless amrita.

"Uphill and to the right of Yamalung, the Terchen performed the reversal ritual of Dorje Trolö for the benefit of the teachings and the general welfare of both central Tibet and Kham. A fierce thunder and hailstorm arose. During it, I glimpsed the thirty chieftains of the haughty spirits in the sky.

"When Terchen Rinpoche performed the *Injunction by Samaya of Devas and Rakshasas* on the peak of the Hepori Hill, I was present as one of his assistants. I gained the certainty that he had summoned all the gods and spirits of these billion worlds led by the four great nyens of Tibet, and that they all accepted his vajra samaya.

"When Terchen Rinpoche performed a three-day consecration at Samye, I saw him at times as Guru Rinpoche in nirmanakaya costume; at times as Great Splendor Vajrakumara; and at times as the Wrathful Guru, without a consort, surrounded by the deities of the complete three seats, casting flowers.

"I visited the village of Drakda where Yeshe Tsogyal was born, and saw the lake that appeared at the time of her birth. Because she and Nupchen were born in the same village, knew one another so well, and spent so much time together, I experienced fleeting, dreamlike memories of that time, including such things as how they played together as children. This brought up both nostalgic sadness and intense meditation experience.

"When I went to the village uphill from there, the birthplace of the victor Longchenpa, and saw the image of him kept in the house of his birth, the pure perception of it as Longchenpa himself arose.

"In Draki Yangdzong we performed the protection and reversal rituals of *Yamantaka the Lord of Life* for the benefit of all central Tibet and Kham. The appearances arose of being enclosed by a vajra fortress, of a sudden wind like that which destroys a world, and of many small, malevolent spirits howling as they were killed and cut up. I also remembered that when Nupchen was in that place, he realized that some rakshasas were consuming the rock of the mountain behind it, and liberated them by casting a kila.

"On the night I camped near the Tsangpo River, I dreamed that I entered a red palace of inconceivably fine design and decoration on top of a mountain. In it was the Four-Armed Avalokita, the compassionate tamer of beings, red in color, wearing the samboghakaya costume, brilliantly luminous. Immeasurable devotion arose in me. On the next day, when I reached the ferry crossing, I saw the Potala lit by the light of the rising sun. I gained certainty about my dream of the night before, and the faith that the Dalai Lama, the Lord of Victors Trinlay Gyamtso, was actually Avalokita.

"In the Tölung Valley, I encountered Chetsun Senge Wangchuk in the form of a yogin. He was wearing a loincloth, a cotton shawl, and a soft, floppy hat, and was walking through the village. Coming upon him suddenly, I begged for instruction and held him by his shawl. He pointed his finger at the clear sky and said, 'That's it,' three times. Then he departed with the power of the winds.

"I then stayed in the village containing the family home of Shikpo Lingpa. Early the next morning, that holy being appeared. His hair bound in a topknot, he was wearing monastic robes with a white outer shawl. He said to me, 'I am Shikpo Lingpa.'

"When I then returned to Tsurphu, indications that I was accompanied by the protector Bernakchen arose.

"When I then returned to Lhasa, I saw signs that some laymen and monastics with perverted aspirations were fomenting agitation that would cause controversy within Tibetan Buddhism. However, there is little need to speak of this.

"Then I started to lead the Terchen's encampment back to the east. On our way, I went to see the offering ceremonies at the Drikung Kagyu seat, Densatil. The pure perception of that place as no different from Vajrasana in India, and of the statue of Achi in her temple as the deity herself, arose. I saw things differently from others. In particular, recollecting the holy Gar Chödingwa's taming of vicious nagas and other haughty beings both with and without form, my devotion blazed. In dreams it became clear that I should go to Drikung Tidrom. However, because of the need to supervise the safe arrival of the Terchen's household at his residence, I didn't go.

"When we reached Nakshö Bengar, in the clouds to the south I suddenly saw an old lama, bluish with a rosy complexion, holding a book. Thinking that he was Lord Bengar Jampal Zangpo, I repeatedly prayed for the unmistaken realization of mahamudra. Just past that place, I saw a pale, bald lama wearing monastic robes. I thought he might be Tratsangwa.

"From the bridge of Khyungpo Seri, I saw the mountains of Nakshö, and had the thought that there was a great guru there somewhere. However, I wasn't free to investigate.

"When we reached the juncture of three valleys at Puzo, I saw nagas in the pools there.

"When we camped at the foot of a mountain to the left of Zegyal that was reputed to be a residence of Vajrasadhu, a young boy wearing an inside-out goatskin with feathers stuck into his hair came to me. He seemed delighted to see me, and promised to provide for our needs. We then reached Neten

Monastery safely. I remained there for a few days, and then came home. On my way, at the crossing of Dagyü Kude, I saw all the local spirits, led by Nabun Genyen, assembled to welcome me back. I safely arrived at Surmang Tashi Lhundrup Ling, my home, and was welcomed by Jampal Gyaltsen, the lama of Nanangtse, and his brother who presented abundant gifts in celebration of my safe return. They asked me to sing of the experiences that arose within me on my journey to central Tibet. In response, I offered the following:

"Courageous sons of the siddhas
Bearing the flower of three-fold faith in your hearts,
With kind words of yearning
You've given this aimlessly wandering yogin
Who's returned from the central region
A feast of delights and stainless, fine scarves.
I'm pleased by this auspicious celebration.
You asked, 'While wandering aimlessly from
    place to place,
What outer and inner wonders did you see?
Tell us of all in song!'
This old boy will answer your question.

"From the original land of the ground, dharmata,
I saw the child of awareness set out,
Drawn by the illusion of appearances.
He entered the house of craving and conception.
He became exhausted climbing the stairs of formation.
Wrapped up in habits, he went to sleep.
When he awoke,
He became distracted by illusory appearances.

When his body, the form of bewilderment, had matured,
He played with the distractions of the six senses.

"I was discouraged by the sight of birth,
And came to despise the illusion of how we're born.
I put away the cause of birth
And sent forth the spy of no-birth.
I put him where he could spy unseen.
Now, I think I need not fear birth.

"When the house of the composite is demolished,
And the rainbow of the body's four elements vanishes,
The dreams of pleasure and pain are experienced.
The old man who's traveled for so long is drunk.

"I saw the difficulty of age and death.
Saddened by the sight of death,
I searched for supreme immortality.
The mist of this life and the next dissolved into the sky.
I entered the expanse, the impregnable fortress
of immortality.
I saw that the designs of the composite were exhausted.
Even if I die right now, my mind is settled.

"Those are the wonders I saw—birth and death.
These magical appearances are like a great optical illusion.
The bewilderment of the bardo is a clever deception.
These are all just like being fooled by a dream.

"The spectacle of the six senses can include anything.
After the six senses and their objects have met,

The immediate mind takes over.
The great wind of the six consciousnesses blows.
The garbage of good and bad karma piles up,
Held by the net of the all-basis.
The result is the habit of samsara.
Temporary spectacles of all kinds can appear.
When the mind takes up pleasure and rejects pain,
The endless terror of samsara has begun.

"But in the bardo between this life and the next,
The powerful hero, the clear light,
Rides swiftly on the steed of method, the illusory body.
He holds the sharp sword of equal taste
And the lance of yogic discipline.
He draws the bow and arrow of means and discernment,
    bliss-emptiness.
He carries the provisions of samadhi.
He brings along emptiness and compassion as companions.
He is unafraid of temporary bewilderment.

"This yogin, a warrior of awareness-display,
Went to central Tibet last year.
I was delighted by the sight of many supreme images.
I saw people from India, Nepal, and Kashmir.
I met supreme incarnate lamas, masters,
And the great sanghas of dharma foundations.
In Kyishö a female spirit created illusions.
In Tsethang I met terrestrial dakinis,
And at Gampo, Gampopa himself.
I saw a mandala in the sky of Tsaritra,
And, in a town there, a ganachakra of place-born dakinis.

I met the celestial dakinis all at once.
I taught causality to maras and barbarians.
In Zangri, I saw the dakini Machik Lapdrön
Dancing in samboghakaya form.
In a dream in Flower Field
I heard predictions in the sound of a stream.
In the Spirit Lake of the Empress of the Desire Realm
I saw her wondrous palace and park,
The wild swirling of a black wind,
And her mule trotting to and fro.
At the gate to Tsangrong, I saw Thangtong Gyalpo,
White like a conch, the size of a mountain.
In sacred places, at passes, in valleys, on
mountains, and by lakes,
I saw innumerable yidams, dharmapalas, male
and female protectors,
And more—in meditation, in dreams, in pure
perception, and in my mind.
I received countless predictions.
In Yömo I saw a feast of heroes,
And received predictions from place-born dakinis.
That is a summary of the wonders I saw.
But I also saw assemblies of faithful disciples,
The directionless conduct of yogins, and more—
All the wonders of the whole land.

"I like singing songs of equal taste.
It is amazing that the deer of our bewildered minds
are drawn to
The mirage of the appearances of this life.
I have seen still other wonders—

The charnel grounds of the sacred places in external
appearance
And the cities of dakinis within the internal
channels and winds!
I have tasted the ganachakra of the protector dakinis.
I've seen, I've seen, I've seen and not seen.
Really, I've seen there is nothing to see.
I've seen the nature of the buddha of ground.
I've seen the appearance of bodies and wisdom.
I've seen wonders beyond exaggeration and denial.

"Really, while this yogin wandered through the land,
While I went to all those places,
Only boundless purity appeared to my mind.
I never experienced anything impure.
Beyond that the visions, pure appearances and clear
appearances
I experienced in those places are too many to recount.

"In this context of human birth,
These are the appearances to my undistracted six senses.
These are the outer and inner wonders I've seen.
Your question was sincere, so I've answered it honestly.
I have sung this for everyone,
Although the suspicious may call me a charlatan.

"That is this yogin's spontaneous song,
An offering of talk about the nature of things.
Please take it as enjoyable music.
Through the virtue of this, may all beings of the three times
Acquire the seed of awakening.

"I composed that spontaneously and gave it to them in writing.

"The Terchen went to Karma Monastery and subsequently summoned me there as well. While we were there, in the Snake Year, my companion gave birth, in the town of Marchok, to a boy with remarkable marks and signs.[49] Terchen Rinpoche said he was the rebirth of Ngedön of Lithang, and gave him the name Orgyen Kunzang Dorje. I came to think that he was an emanation of Lachen Gongpa Rapsel. Taklung Ma Rinpoche said that he was an emanation of Kawa Paltsek. Whoever's rebirth he is, he certainly isn't the rebirth of a donkey! This son of mine has accomplished benefit for the teachings and beings visible to all. I don't think more than that is necessary.

"Then the Terchen went to his newly established seat, Tsike Norbu Sumdo, to tame the earth there. I went as well, and in the company of Drongyak Tingdzin Zangpo, a predicted disciple of the Terchen, performed *The Great Offering to the Eight Classes of Gods and Spirits* and *The Proclamation of Samaya to Gods and Spirits.* During this, I saw Begyal as a blue man riding a blue horse, holding a lance-banner, and I saw the god of Tsike Norbu, appearing as a yaksha holding a club crested by a jewel, riding a garuda, with fearsome tsens on his right, male and female devas on his left, and naga water-lords before him. They all received the vajra samaya.

"In that same place, the Terchen bestowed *The Great Perfection Heart-Drop of Samantabhadra.* During this, I actually perceived him as Samantabhadra Vajradhara.

"I then returned home. While at Surmang, I requested a divination from Ramgo Jampal. After performing it, he requested a vajra song. I offered a description of my experience of Lhasa, in central Tibet, as a pure realm as follows:

"A HO! This beggar, this yogin—I, Barway Dorje—
Went to see the sacred places in the middle of
the land.
When I was at the seat of the glorious Lord
Tsalpa,
At the end of the night, in the last of my sleep,
While my mind was a mix of sleep and
clear light,
I saw a beautiful realm in the west,
In it a mountain and on its peak
A three-storied palace of jewels
In a tent of rainbows.
In the center of this transparent palace,
On a lovely and precious throne, lotus, sun,
and moon,
I saw seated the glorious Avalokita.
This was mixed with the sight of central
Lhasa itself,
Which spontaneously appeared as a pure realm.
I gained conviction that the Lord Dalai Lama,
Vajradhara,
Is Avalokita himself.
The victors, our refuge, emanate through
compassionate skill.
They manifest inconceivable variety for the taming
of beings.
This is hard for the foolish and infantile to fathom.

So don't make partisan distinctions;
Let your devotion be impartial and all-inclusive.
May all keep this in mind.

"I then returned to Tsike, and undertook the task of building the residence there. Just after that, however, we lost Terchen Rinpoche; he turned his thought to the needs of others, and passed away.[50] I went immediately to Neten Monastery and took charge of the presentation of offerings and the making of supplications. After that, in the service of his consort and children, I performed the protection, reversal, and eradication rituals of the Rishi Loktripala. During that time, in a mixture of meditation and sleep, an old woman with no eyes appeared, waving her hands and attended by a lot of female beggars. I prayed to Great Splendor Vajrakumara. As the display of his compassion, from space descended a Supreme Son, with a kila blade, red-hot like a meteor, as his lower body.[51] He burnt them all to ashes.

"For the funeral ceremony, I made an image of the Terchen. On the evening I finished it, everyone present saw three sudden rains of grain. I think it was the Lord Terchen himself blessing and casting flowers upon the image. After that, I went to Ga to fundraise for a golden container for Terchen Rinpoche's relics. On my way, below Dela, I encountered Padma Tensung, surrounded by a lot of ghosts, and followed by a lot of grey dogs. At Palkhyimye I developed a naga ailment. By the time I reached Shendzong Monastery I was tormented by infected blisters. One night, just before dawn, a woman wearing white clothing appeared to me and said, 'Combine in equal amounts the eight planetary medicines and the nine-headed planetary medicine with traces of the following spirit-repellants: black agaru, the flesh of someone killed by a weapon, gugul, the flesh of a tilo, the wings of a kyang-bird, and nardostachys grandiflora. If you consume this mixture and also burn some, it will alleviate your illness.'

"On the next day Lama Nyinje Ötro assembled the ingredients she specified. I ate them and was quickly freed from sickness. This was instruction from Shrimala, the goddess of medicine. If this prescription were adapted to suit each type of illness, such as those of the blood and those of the gall, it would serve as an extremely profound remedy for the illnesses of our time.

"At the ancestral home of Khamtrul Rinpoche, the residence of the Gyawa family of Jomnyak, I met both the supreme guide Kunga Tendzin and Khamtrul Chökyi Nyima in a dream. When I saw the statue depicting Lord Mitrijnana in the temple at the stupa in Jomnyak, I saw it as his actual wisdom body.

"Traveling by way of Druda, by the mountain to the right of Lapda, I encountered Lord Tsongkapa, Lozang Drakpa, with his two heart-sons. Their bodies were the size of mountains.

"At Thalung Monastery Anye Chözang told me that the offering ritual for the Glorious Goddess written by Gyatsen Tulku Ngawang Tarchin was hard to chant every day, and asked me to write a briefer one. That night, after dark but before the stars had appeared, I saw a dark blue woman with a ferocious demeanor, riding side-saddle on a pale yellow mule. So on the next day I wrote an offering ritual.

"While traveling east by way of Dungkor, on the side of Mount Paru, which is considered a residence of the activity protector called the Atsara, I saw an old atsara-yogin.[52] When I later returned home, the Atsara told me that he had performed the activity ensuring my safe return that year. Some of my monks saw two monks, one old and one young, taking turns watching our animals.

"Once again, on the face of Dalung Yarna Rock, I saw Lord Lozang Drakpa. Later, a self-arisen image of that lord appeared on that rock.

"In the service of the entire region of Ga, I convened a Great Accomplishment Assembly of *Tukdrup Barchay Kunsel* in the Kamjo Temple. During it, I saw the trikaya of Guru Rinpoche many times. Rigo Lama Jampal served as the Vajra Regent for the ritual. I came to think he might be the rebirth of a monk from Zahor who attended the Great Abbot Shantarakshita when he came to Tibet. That and other vague recollections arose in me at that time. There was a demonic spirit inhabiting that area. I compelled him through samadhi, and he went elsewhere. Before he did so, however, he struck me on the cheek in resentment. It hurt for a month.

"While I was staying in the town of Chiwo, I met Rigo Lama Yishin, who was circumambulating to alleviate his dropsy. The thought arose in me that he would live for another three years, and he did.

"Previously, while I was painting the murals at Dechentse, Chöpen Drinzang and the four other protector dakinis had appeared to me and promised to perform the activity of power. Starting from the time when I received the empowerment of Kurukulle from Zuru Tenkyong, I saw her many times. The words of her sadhana arose spontaneously from the lake of my all-basis, but I remained neutral toward them. Eventually, however, predictions came to Lama Karma Jana of Shendzong Monastery in dreams, and he earnestly encouraged me. So I wrote down *The Padmadakini Sadhana* that I had received as a mind treasure, and gave the empowerment and transmission. This was the first of the profound dharmas that it has been my honor to reveal.

"Lama Karma Jinpa performed the approach and accomplishment, and experienced the usual signs. Especially, one night a woman gave him a piece of coral, which was unmarked by holes and the size of the first joint of one's forefinger, which he gave to me.

"I went to Karma Monastery, bearing extensive offerings, and presented them to the Terchen's consort and sons. With these, we were able to create an eight-foot high receptacle of gold to contain the Terchen's relics.

"I went to Tsike Monastery to continue the construction there, and served as the lama-assistant to Tersay Rinpoche, the Terchen's son. At Danyin Kalarongo, I saw on several occasions a water-lord, green in color, his head and whole body covered with eyes.

"In the service of the Kingdom of Nangchen, I performed the reversal ritual of the Eight Dispensations. At its conclusion, when I was performing the entrustment and dispersal at Genyen Dzongnak, I saw a water-lord, who appeared as a white-colored man wearing armor of conch shell, with a lot of snakes emerging from his helmet. His upper body was out of the water, and he appeared pleased.

"I then gave the Empowerment of the Eight Dispensations called *The Lotus Crystal Cave* to a crowd of almost ten thousand people from the area around Riwoche. At first, a brawl occurred. I recited the dharani for the pacification of anger, and the fighting stopped. I convened the Amrita Accomplishment ritual of *Tukdrup Barchay Kunsel* at the Nyingma College there, during which I briefly saw a stream of undefiled amrita descend from the bodies of the deities above the amrita vessel.

"In the Trakhyilma Temple, I presented thousand-fold offerings to the three deities of life. During this I saw, for a long time, their three wisdom bodies.

"When I consecrated the image of Vaishravana at the Shapdrung Ladrang, slight signs, such as the radiation of red light, appeared.

"When I circumambulated the palace of Chakrasamvara on the mountain behind the monastery, the pure appearance of the viras and dakinis of the sacred places and lands arose filling the ground, sky, and horizon. Everyone else present saw a lot of vultures flying about.

"I then returned to my own area and went into retreat at

Marchokze. While there I gave the empowerment and transmission of my mind treasure, *Padmadakini,* to Tsering Gönpo, the retreatant of Shartse. While he was performing the approach and accomplishment, a lot of pleased-looking red women wearing fine jewelry appeared to him. As well, a lot of white women wearing white veils and holding books appeared. They asked him why he was not chanting their sadhana, which was the book they were carrying. They seemed offended. He told me that these dreams had occurred repeatedly, and provided me with paper. In that way, he opened wide the gate of auspiciousness, and so, for the first time, I wrote down on paper *The Dakini Cycle* that I had kept secret for twenty-four years. This was the one I had found at Dorje Zom, in the same region. At the time of that discovery, I had been accompanied by Kachö Wangmo—the rebirth of Palgyi Chönema—who was predicted by Guru Rinpoche to be my companion. In response to what Tsering Gönpo told me I now performed the feast, saw the face of Vajrayogini, and received her blessing. I thereafter gave the empowerment and transmission, for the first time and secretly, to about ten novices and monks with pure aspirations, including the person who had first asked me to write it down. At that time, I repeatedly saw Guru Rinpoche, father and mother, in actuality and in meditation experience. They revealed the meaning of the profound symbols. I also saw the protectors of treasure, such as the protector dakinis, in their own forms. They received the vajra commitment.

"From that time on I began to gradually give this empowerment and transmission to all who considered themselves my disciples. The root dharma holders are Ma Rinpoche, Lho Rinpoche, and Jedrung Rinpoche—the Three Named Ratna. I also transmitted it carefully to Drongyül Rinpoche, Orgyen Nüden Dorje, and others. Many people, more than I have room to mention, achieved remarkable signs through its approach and accomplishment.

"Then, on the upper floor of my companion's family home, I received *The Peaceful and Wrathful Ones of the Spacious Expanse* and *The Treasure Guardian Cycle;* these were written down by the solitary mantra-holder Drala. I gave the image of Guru Rinpoche called *Source of all Siddhi* to my brother, its predicted recipient, Kyodrak Tentrul Rinpoche. This was the image that I had made from the bodhichitta of Guru Rinpoche, father and mother, and gold dust that I had found at the Lotus Crystal Cave at Dzomnang. I needed the image that I had previously given him for my reception of treasure, and therefore asked for it back; he returned it to me.

"At that time, as had been predicted, at the oncoming of summer, when the Queen of Spring is calling us, I went to reveal the supreme residence of the Magical Peaceful and Wrathful Ones, Surmang Dalkyap. The people of the area provided excellent support. We began with a feast and a smoke offering. Then, accompanied by about thirty disciples, I went in search of treasure. On the side of Utse Rock, I found the bones of Prince Mune Tsenpo, which had been concealed there by the ministers Drugu Ebaksha, Bhami Trishir, and five others. They did so at the command of Guru Rinpoche, who told them to bury the prince's remains on the face of a mountain in Kham 'like a soaring white garuda.' I knew that this was Dalkyap Mountain, and discovered the bones, along with a zi stone offered to Guru Rinpoche by Dunkhyong the naga king, and especially relics of the Tathagatha Ashokashri that were the size of a thirteen-year-old boy's fist.

"I also sent my son, Padma Tsewang; my ritual assistant, Karma Mönlam; my attendant Menlha; and others into the sacred place, having told them what to do. In a practice cave of Guru Rinpoche's that had his hand and footprints, they found some of his clothing. On the right and left of the mountain's peak shaped like a lion leaping into the sky, they found twenty-five types of samaya substance, such as amrita consecrated individually by the eight vidyadharas of India through the practice of their respective dispensations. Behind that, in the practice cave of Yeshe Tsogyal, they found a lamp of turquoise, a mongoose made of turquoise, an image of the thousand-armed Avalokita made by Guru Rinpoche, a stupa, and her handprints in white stone, which they also delivered to me. At that time, the waving of silk ribbons by dakinis in front of the place and in the practice caves, the appearance of rainbows, and a rain of flowers were seen by all. I identified the things that had been found there, and wrote a guide to the place and a list of the discoveries. In a state of heightened faith and delight, we left.

"After that, while traveling to gather dairy products, we camped in Dorje Zamlung. That night, a woman, who seemed to be the one who had predicted my discovery of the dakini treasure, appeared to me wearing a robe and jacket of white wool decorated by rainbow-colored felt. Her hair was unbound, and she wasn't wearing much jewelry. Accompanied by two other similar women she approached me and with a pleased and affectionate expression said, 'It is now time for me to entrust you with the treasure of Kyodrak. Travel by way of the narrow streambed on the other side of Zangmuk Pass, and I will give it to you.'

"On the next day I offered a golden drink and prepared to travel.[53] I rested before we reached the pass and sent a monk ahead to see if it was passable. He returned and said that there was a footpath, so I sent the others with the horses and mules around the mountain, and I took the footpath through the pass. In the shadow of a rock shaped like a finger, I saw what appeared to be a hand beckoning me onward. I walked toward the rock and saw the women I had encountered the night before standing behind it. Their leader handed me a chest. It was made of stone and lined with wax, and was shaped like a jointed section of bamboo. She said to me, 'This will accomplish everything.' Then they disappeared among the rocks.

"I thought that there might be further treasures there, but felt too hurried to search for them. The chest contained *The Manjushri Yamantaka Cycle.*

"When I returned to Surmang, I received a letter of divination about entering retreat from Lama Yishin Norbu of Rigo. In reply, I offered him this song describing my state using the four impossibilities as images, as a pleasing and wondrous offering-cloud:[54]

> "Dharmakaya Yogini, bless me!
>
> "You bring joy to all who live.
> You have understood all outer and inner things.

With homage of the three gates, I respectfully address
The lotus feet of the guru with eight-fold mastery.[55]

"As medicine for eyes afflicted by this five-fold
degeneration,[56]
You have appeared, according to your wishes, Yishin,
In a supreme form like a sky-jewel, Norbu,[57]
The full mandala of marks and signs.
I am greatly inspired by your rescue of disciples.

"I am well but use up the result of past virtue
By chasing after poisonous offerings and wandering
through villages.
I tell myself this is altruistic, but it is really just selfishness.
I feel sorry for myself, but there is nothing to be done.

"Nevertheless, at all times in this bardo of birth and death,
Having cut through the complexities of the three times,
I remain at ease.
I rest easily in the unaltered nature. The dream of thoughts,
Like the child of a childless woman calling to the east
and west
From the top of a mountain, is over.

"I sit slumped having resolved that all these appearances
are illusions.
Things have no nature. I drink the saliva of elephants
From a begging bowl made of rabbit-horn.

"In a single meditation session, this yogin of simplicity
Ended all the complexities of this life.

With not a speck of anything to do, I put on a saffron
blanket
Woven from tortoise-hair.

"If you have no hope or fear, you have no need for
fruition.
That which is attained and the attainment of it
are purified,
Like the ornamental kamala flowers of the sky.

"I have written this as a design in a dream,
Employing the four impossibilities as images.
May it be a pleasing offering-cloud PUJAH HO!
With the prayer that we meet again soon, with divine
fabric,
And with the two precious things, this was sent from
the monastery and offered
By the one with three-fold perception called Raktrul.

"At around the same time, Lama Jampal Gyaltsen wrote me a letter. At the end of my reply, I wrote the following, a spontaneously-composed reminder of the nature:

"A HO! Thinking of nothing, all is mind.
If you think of all, there is nothing at all.
If you are not isolated from the complexities of mind,
Physical and verbal isolation are just temporary.
Mental isolation is like the child of a childless woman,
Nothing more than a name.
All complexity is pacified in simplicity.
Anything can emerge from simplicity.

Mind and appearances are not two.
There is no meditation and not even an instant's
distraction.
Inseparable bliss and emptiness are mahamudra.
If you can't grasp complexity,
How can you grasp what you think of as simplicity?
Spin the all-pervasive wheel of simplicity.
Cut through the net of complexity's characteristics
With the sword of the wisdom of simplicity.
Once the seal of samsara, nirvana, and the path is
broken,
The hidden deception of positive and negative
causality is exposed.
Natural, spontaneously present, A LA LA!

"Then I painted the murals on the west wall of the Trakhyilma Temple at Surmang. While doing so, I depicted the precious mahasiddha Mase Lodrö Rinchen, his four consorts, Joden Lodrö Drakpa, Surmang Karma Tenpa, and others as I had seen them in visions. Therefore they were all depicted as they really appeared. Because Tendzin Gelek Nyima was a teacher of mine, and because Surmang Trungpa Rinpoche had recently passed away in a nomad community, I depicted them as well.

"Then the holy Tersay went to Drakyap with me as his assistant. On the night we went to the lake below Drugu Lhadrak, I remembered how Guru Rinpoche had camped there one summer along with ten disciples with pure karma. One night, while I was performing ceremonies for the benefit of the leader of Drakyap, I became distracted by the sight of a large image of Buddha Shakyamuni that was suddenly visible from the temple. This was caused by the spirit of the place. On another night, the spirit appeared in the form of Guru Rinpoche. I compelled it through samadhi and it disappeared.

"When I performed the reversal ritual of the Eight Dispensations, the wisdom deities appeared in the sky. It seemed to me that the ceremony would be of great service to all of Tibet.

"Through the mischief of the mountain goddess of Drakyap, I contracted white pox and came close to death.[58] I had my attendant Gyurme plant a banner on the mountain's peak and offer cleansing smoke and a golden drink. One night I dreamed that I caught hold of a woman by her clothing. She struggled like a dog straining at the leash, but I held on and prayed to my guru and yidam. From the sky, a glowing kila of red-hot iron fell on her and burnt her up. Starting then, I gradually recovered.

"When I returned to my homeland, I felt that I was being followed by many spirits of the previous region. I built a little house on top of four piled boulders, filled it with ransom offerings, and dedicated it to them. I then generated my yidam and dissolved him into a marker stone, in that way creating a boundary. After that, no one appeared.

"When I watched the Tenth-Day Dance at Khamgar, I felt the faith and certainty that I had reached the Glorious Copper-Colored Mountain.

"As I went by way of Yukshe Sun Pass, and along the peaks, I was welcomed by the spirits of the area. Around that time, a bridge at Kela started to fall down. I performed consecration and the entrustment of activity to the Realm Protectors, and nothing bad happened. I also saw indications of the passing of Garwang Rinpoche.

"At Tsike, the great Tenth-Day Dance of *Tukdrup Barchay Kunsel* was convened. I gained the certainty that through the blessings of holy beings such as Tsewang Norbu, the Great Vidyadhara of Kathok; the Vidyadhara Rölpai Dorje; and especially through that of the Terchen and his son the place had become a pure realm like Chamaradvipa.

"I returned to Surmang and performed the offering ceremonies in connection with the passing of Garwang Rinpoche. One night I dreamed that he advised me, at length, of the importance of taking responsibility for the teachings of Surmang.

"One day I performed the accomplishment of prosperity according to my own treasures. That night, a man riding a blue horse appeared to me. The next morning, when my attendant brought my early tea, he found a small leather pouch by my bed. He asked me what it was; I asked him what was in it. He shook it and said, 'Something heavy is rolling around in it. The top is tied shut.'

"I examined it carefully. It was a pouch made of rhinoceros hide containing a pleasing brown stone, round and bound by woolen threads. I put it aside and kept on examining it for several days, but was unable to figure out what it was. About two weeks after that, I dreamed that four men—white, brown, blue, and yellow in color, wearing fine garments, and riding horses of their respective colors—came to me and said, 'We are the four great nyens. We have already given you the wish-fulfilling jewel you wanted. It would be good if you cleansed and venerated it.'

"I asked them about the origin and history of the jewel, but they vanished without answering me. I felt that I really had to know about it, so I performed *Tukdrup* feasts and the earnest entrustment of activity to the dakinis and dharmapalas, but the jewel's story remained unclear.

"A year later, on a night when I was performing a tenth-day feast offering, the protector Shanglön appeared before me, dressed as a king, seated like Maitreya on a small throne.[59] Thinking of him as my guru or Arya Avalokita, I prayed to him. He responded with general conversation for a while, appearing pleased and at ease. Then I asked him about the history of the round stone given me by the four men who claimed to be the four great nyens. He said nothing, so I insisted. He said, 'A wish-fulfilling jewel was taken from the ocean by Indrabhuti, the king of Zahor. Through its power, he discovered Guru Rinpoche, Padma Gyalpo, in the Milky Ocean in the southwest and adopted him as his son. He brought all the countries surrounding his, in all four directions, under his control, and through his veneration and supplication of the jewel, acquired wealth like a sky-treasury. Later, Guru Rinpoche took measures to avoid the kingship, and was exiled to the border regions by the ministers and subjects. His adoptive father, the king, unable to bear their separation, followed him and offered him the wish-fulfilling jewel found in the ocean. He presented it to him as an inheritance and to supply all that he needed—food, wealth, dwelling, and companions. Guru Rinpoche touched the jewel to the top of the king's head and then placed it in the king's left hand. He told him to hold out his right hand, and then spat in it, blessing his saliva so that it became a jewel of peerless radiance and beauty. He said, "As you have no son, accept this in place of a son."

" 'That jewel was given the name Precious Radiant Jewel. King Indrabhuti prayed to it, and the dakini siddha Vinasa came to his land and bore him a son. A long time after that, the kingdom was overthrown. The Tibetan King Songtsen Gampo sent his minister Tönmi Sambhota with two attendants to India to learn both language and dharma. Tönmi remained there for several years. During that time, his servant, called Jaraken, went to a market and saw the jewel created from Guru Rinpoche's saliva in a merchant's stall. He thought, "If I offer this to my king, I will be well rewarded," and bought it with many pieces of gold and silver. When Tönmi and his attendants returned to Tibet, the jewel was offered to Songtsen Gampo, who was very pleased. The king venerated the jewel, enshrining it, and his son, the future King Lungnamtrül, was born. The jewel was renamed Drop of Light. Although the jewel originally appeared to be sapphire, at this time, the end of the age of degeneration, its elements have petrified so that it appears as though made of asmagharbha stone. When the age again becomes a time of waxing virtue, it will once again appear as made of sapphire. Because of the instability of subsequent generations of the line of dharma kings, and because they would die through violence, when Guru Rinpoche came to Tibet he entrusted the jewel to the four great nyens. Now, because you have been blessed by both Arya Avalokita and Manjushri, and because you need to accomplish great deeds in the service of the teachings and beings, it has been offered to you. If you consecrate it by combining the accomplishment of wealth with the accomplishment of the father and mother yakshas, you will quickly accomplish whatever you wish without impediment. Don't forget all this; keep it in mind. I am headed east from here.'

"That vision, a combination of meditation experience and dream, lasted for quite a while. I did all the practices that he had indicated, and my activity flourished. I have offered empowerment to the Fathers and Sons, and the number of my disciples and patrons in both the north and south has steadily increased.[60]

"While I was on my way to Sharda and was in Rongpo Palthang, a handsome, well-dressed young man gave me a small image of the Bhagavat Akshobhya made of bell-metal. I asked who he was, and he pointed to the area of Gyam, saying, 'I'm from up there.'

"He was the local deity Dhoti.

"Also in that place, in the midst of a crowd of people, the dharmapala Red Tsiu gave me dharma king Trisong Detsen's brocade cloak.

"When I was in Pelungpungri an old monk with gray hair, carrying a staff, said to me, 'Up there, in the Dogar Ladrang, is a begging bowl. Within it is a piece of a skull with the form of a wrathful deity painted on it. Go get it; I will tell you its history later.'

"After I found what he had described, the dharmapala Rhino-Hide Armor appeared to me in his own form and said, 'This was a support for the practice of Yamantaka used by Nupchen Sangye Yeshe. He acquired it in India. It depicts Yamantaka the Lord of Life, painted in the Nepali style by the Nepali master Indraratna, on a semicircular piece of the skull of a rishi. It would be good if you used it as a practice support.'

"In Drigyü, a yogin hurriedly handed me a nine-pronged vajra made of yellow bell-metal, saying, 'This was the scepter of the master Mahahumkara.'

"Then the yogin disappeared.

"When I was performing a purification and consecration ceremony in the home of the leader of Deta, from the four directions appeared many male figures, white, yellow, red, and green in color, holding arrows bound with silk and various weapons. They dissolved into the support. When I then performed the feeding of spirits, I saw the spirits of the deceased local leader and all his ancestors appear to actually receive the food.

"It was often said that the local deity of Gugu in western Tridu was the ferocious son of Magyal Pomra. He appeared to me, along with his two brothers. All three of them were ferocious in demeanor. They received samaya and promised from that time onward to perform whatever tasks I assigned them and to guard the area.

"I was met at the Gugu Pass by mounted lamas and monks of Shendzong Monastery. As we were riding together, I remembered all of the major and minor events in the history of the Dzachu River Valley all the way to the place called the Five Ram Brothers, and my own former life as Anu Zikpen, the leader of Takrong.

"I was enthusiastically welcomed by the resident deity of Dzagyal, who appeared as a blue man wearing iron armor riding a blue horse and surrounded by others like himself—by Drenchen Dzamar, by Norbu Karpo, and by other local deities. I wrote a few liturgies for the presentation of offerings to them based on how I perceived them.

"Led by Chankyi Mingyur, the rebirth of Gedrak Sengtruk Adom of Drupgar, the monastery asked me to direct the construction of an enclosing wall. I did so, and saw the local spirits helping by carrying earth and stones. The wall was successfully completed. During the work, I saw in a vision the growth of many trees in the area; this was certainly an indication of the future. I think that nowadays there is no resident deity in Drongdzong, and that the one in Ludzong is virtuous.

"When I went to perform a ceremony to purify the residue of the past war involving the Nine-Hundred Northern Enemies,[61] the Three Chinese Divisions, and so forth, I found the battlefield filled with the ghosts of those killed in battle and with spirits who feed on violence. It was quite spooky, but I gradually pacified the place. When I performed the subduing of enemies by means of Yamantaka, from beneath the ground came a terrifying roar, like thunder, which we all heard. From that time on, there was no further harm caused by the Northern Enemies.

"When I performed a ceremony for the general welfare of Anyeshok, I placed my hand on the head of Raplu, the local leader, and found myself saying, without thinking, 'Today it's my hand, but you'd better make sure from now on that your head isn't covered by Nyatso Purdzong.'

"As I warned him, he and his son were killed by the forces of Nyatso the next year.

"I saw that the mountain there was a residence of wealth gods, and that there were a few material treasures there, but circumstances did not allow me to extract them.

"I ended up traveling clockwise around the mountain, and came to Strict Golden Hill, where there were so many ghosts of people who had died violently that I thought there would be further violence there.

"At the request of Megöl Gyünma, I praised the local deity Lering Dungmar Taktse. Because he is half mara and half tsen, he gave rise to disturbances in order to challenge me. Although the sky was clear everywhere else, above my tent were gathered dark clouds from which smoke appeared to issue forth. This lasted the length of time it takes to drink a cup of tea. Since I knew what this meant, I fumigated with mantra. Suddenly, there came a thunderclap loud enough to split one's brain, a terrifying burst of lightning, and a dangerous hailstorm. I subdued all this through visualization and meditated on a protection-circle, and it all stopped without anyone being harmed.

“I also brought under samaya all the other local deities of Upper Dza, great and small, such as those of Karong and Tongku, Pentri Zurshi Taktse, Lekhyim Pawo Taktse, Pamo Yutse, Trayi Tokdzong, the Three Brothers of Traram, Khampa Yaknying, and Domja Marmo.

“Because we were related on my father’s side, I thought it would be beneficial if the leader of Nyatso became my patron, but his mind was turned against me by a few laymen and monks, and it didn’t happen.

“I went to Jakok to fulfill the wishes of the community and of specific individuals. In front of Jowo Gyokchen Dong Mountain, because I was told there were spirit disturbances in the area, I performed a cleansing smoke offering. As the four great nyens of Tibet originated there, it is a place of strict samaya, where activity is accomplished without specific injunction being necessary.

“A patron gave me a blue yak. It died suddenly one night. Because it was the rebirth of a Mongolian bull, and might therefore have become vicious, it was liberated by the dharmapalas.

“When I performed praise of the dralas’ bravery, from the side of the mountain appeared five wolves making all kinds of sounds. I recognized this to be a sign of Ekajati’s presence.

"On the way back, at Drupgar, I performed the presentation of ransom to ghosts and samaya-corruptors. That night the monk Tendzin Puntsok and others dreamed that, on the back of a huge black bear, the size of the whole region, was a vicious rakshasi and a lot of other spirits. Among them were a few people, known to the dreamers, who had died in that area. They were all headed east by way of Jangda.

"The contagious illness that had been afflicting the region was pacified, clearly indicating, as did their dream, that the malevolent spirit responsible had gone elsewhere.

"Because the crops were poor that year at Shendzong Monastery and throughout the region, and because there was also a lack of dairy products, there was danger of famine, and I was asked to intervene. I set up a ragged white tent below the monastery and performed a ceremony for the propitiation of local deities. While I was beginning the main body of the ceremony, an old man unknown to anyone suddenly appeared. When asked his name, he said it was Lamdro Puntsok, 'Abundant Success.' He was given food and drink, and then disappeared taking with him the offerings for the local deities. I think he was the local spirit, actually appearing among us to receive the offerings. Thereafter, the grain and dairy yield in that region increased; the outcome was a happy one.

"While I was staying with the Lhabu family in Dzeda, the activity protector Atsara, who is revered in that region and simply called 'the male god,' appeared to me in actuality as an elderly monk with a beard and eyebrows as white as a conch. The ends of his long shawl were knotted. He promised to perform entrusted activity. On the next day I made a representation of him and gave it to the family.

"One night I suddenly awoke from sleep in a state of considerable excitement. My room was filled with smoke and there was an unpleasant smell of something burning. I thought there must be a fire and called my attendant, who assured me that there was no fire. I knew it to be the mischief of spirits, so I compelled them with the samadhi of my yidam. After an interval of various vague appearances, a small area clear of smoke appeared adjacent to my pillow. From within this, a voice said, 'From now on, when you are in the north, I'll go south; when you are in the south, I'll go north.'

"I felt that this was Padma Tenkyong's doing.

"After breakfasting on wheat-meal, I went on and saw, on the side of a great rock, the deity Gyokchen Dongra who appeared as a large, impressive, vigorous-looking man wearing a cloak of white silk, seated at ease on a throne.

"When I performed a feast offering in order to form a connection with the sacred place Yudrak, I saw among the rocks a colorful tent of rainbow light filled with the forms of deities and with larger and smaller drops of light. I noticed that the small lake there had absorbed the blessing of the amrita in Guru Rinpoche's skull-cup.

"When I circumambulated Nakyöl Tashi Lhatse, I indistinctly saw Vajrasadhu in his own form, that of a red blacksmith. I became certain that he guards that place, and it clearly appeared to me that it is a residence of Hayagriva.

"I served a feast of dharma teaching to all the virtuous and fortunate men and women of the area, according to the wants and needs of each. When I was on the point of leaving to return to my homeland, Tsering Yangdzom, a woman of authentic family connected to me by activity and great affection, unable to bear our parting, demonstrated her yearning through gesture, loving words, and facial expressions. I too felt sad at the prospect of our parting. In that state of intense sadness, I spontaneously composed the following as my departing message:

"KYE HO! Listen, fortunate one!
First, you were born in a good family.
Your birth is not inferior; you were born as a dakini.
But then you were cast into the crowd of the worldly,
And were somewhat corrupted by vulgar bewilderment.
You were contaminated by the breath of demonic friends.
However, your actions were good; you are devoted
to dharma.
You met a holy, qualified guru.
You tasted the amrita of instruction.
You are fortunate to have met me.

"This yogin isn't saying this to praise himself.
I met the lord guru in my youth.
I then studied as well as I could.
Finally, I devoted myself to practice,
Meditating on profound generation and completion.

The signs of the path of channels, winds, and drops arose.
I bear the signs of a vira of authentic family,
Connection with whom is meaningful.
That is why meeting me has been the timely awakening
Of a karmic connection from past lives,
Maintained by good aspirations.

"After we made a physical connection,
You never saw me as a lover, but as a guru.
You were definitely born with the mahayana disposition.

"After we began to converse,
You never saw it as talk, but as instruction.
You are definitely a vessel for profound dharma.

"When we cultivated our skill in bliss-emptiness,
Your faith and affection blazed like fire.
It is certain that our connection is due to past karma.

"Now, we shall not meet for a while.
You have said, 'I require instruction!'
Those words, spoken by you in love, have moved me.
I'll summarize the essential points of practice.

"Listen, qualified one of authentic family,
Young woman linked to me by our hearts,
Supreme companion in the achievement of great bliss!

"Having trained your being through the common
preliminaries,
Accumulate and purify through the uncommon ones.

Always meditate on your body as that of the deity,
And on all appearances as the deity's form.
That will purify physical wrongs and veils,
And bring about the arising of undifferentiated pure appearances.

"Meditate on all utterance of speech as the sound of mantra.
That will purify verbal wrongs and veils,
And bring about the natural accomplishment of the three roots.

"Look at your mind, self-awareness.
Has it substance, color, shape, or characteristic?
If not, look to see where it is—inside or outside.
If you don't find it, look to see if it is the one who's looking.
If it is, look at what is searching.
If it isn't, look at what is aware.
Look to see if experience and thought are two.
If there are no looked-at and looker,
That is what is called the 'mind's empty nature.'

"Experience doesn't stop.
Look to see where thoughts first arise;
Then where they remain, come, and go;
And finally, where they end and are destroyed.
Looking, you don't see anything.
Like a water-moon or a mirror's reflection,
Appearance-emptiness and clarity-emptiness are each indivisible.

This has been the mind's nature from the
beginning.
Looking at it now, you resolve that it has.

"Then, when you apply this in meditation,
You see it just by thinking, 'I shall look at my mind.'
If there is no directed focus, let go in that.
There is nothing to see; don't search for something.
There being nothing to be meditated on is itself the
absolute truth.
Don't engage in the intellect's spying.
The experience of nothing to be done, beyond the
intellect, is authentic.
Whatever occurs, rest in that state.
Take the absence of good and bad on the path.
Being without acceptance and rejection is the conduct,
Without any hope or fear, stopping or creating.
The ordinary, unaltered mind is revealed.
That is the beginning of the gradual result.

"In support of this, for correction and enhancement,
Don't allow generation and completion, the boat
to liberation,
To develop the leak of procrastination.
Apply the sealant that is the recollection of there
being no leisure.
Don't lose the oars of diligence, which maintain
The path's speed, in the waves of attachment.
Give rise to exertion through the recollection of death.
With heart-felt devotion, entrust yourself utterly
To the guru, the undeceiving captain,

And be free of capriciousness.
While still not liberated from samsara's ocean,
Fear the crocodiles of bad karma.
Beware the mischief of relatives, the fish and beavers.
Through birth, the poisonous belly of the frog opens wide.
Sickness is a fish thrashing about on hot sand.
Aging is a snake slithering through a valley.
The taste of death is unavoidable.
The horns of death, the water buffalo, are sharp.
So don't be attached to samsara.
It's time to reach the dry land of liberation.
Therefore be diligent without distraction.

"As well, whatever signs you experience,
Don't get excited; that's a great mara.
Whatever agitation and suffering arise,
They are just temporary side effects; look at
their nature.
Whatever joy and pleasure arise,
Regard them as the guru's kindness.
That will cause your merit to increase and be
inexhaustible.
Whatever undesired misery arises,
Believe it to be past karma.
That will sweep away wrongs and downfalls.
Never carelessly denigrate
Any aspect of the three jewels.
Don't get lost in negativity and antipathy.
Meditate on impartial compassion
For our parents, all beings of the three realms.
Dedicate your virtue to beings.

"If you practice all of this, not abandoning it,
The roots of dharma are complete.
The essence of meditation is complete.
This has been my experience.
These are my instructions to you.
They are undeceiving, young one.
Liberation of your mind is certain, one of
authentic family.
These words were written at the request
Of my dear friend with the signs of a dakini,
Named Tsering,
By a yogin crowned with a topknot,
Given by matrikas and dakinis of the expanse the name
Pal Traktung Barway Dorje,
At the dharma camp of Tashi Ling,
In one session break.
I dedicate all virtue to beings;
May they attain omniscient buddhahood.

"I presented her with that and also gave her some experiential instruction in the two stages. She saw her own face, the single dharmakaya, and recited three hundred million of the six syllables; she became a yogini who had definitely found her way to the path.

"She is an example of the almost fifty women of authentic family with whom I formed a physical connection. I don't think you could say that my touch bestows liberation, but I always did my best to plant the seed of liberation in my companions. They all have engaged in the usual virtuous actions. Especially, they all recognized the connate wisdom of bliss-emptiness;

each of them became able to maintain a good level of experience. I have at least, beyond doubt, helped them that much.

"As for my behavior in this connection, I was never uncontrolled in my three gates and never cavalier or uncaring. I always applied, in my own experience, the profound secret instructions that came from that treasury of such, the mind of Orgyen Chokgyur Dechen Lingpa. In every instance I definitely experienced, like rock meeting bone, what he taught me. I have no shame, in either the social or moral sense, about having correctly put into practice what was taught me by both deities and gurus. My experience of the profound vajra path gave rise to heartfelt certainty of the view and meditation; I am fit to be in the ranks of longhaired yogins dressed in white.

"Then, on my way back home I went to gather grain in Nangchen Dagyü. During this time, I met Orgyen Nüden Dorje, Lhodrong Tulku, by Dokham Frog Lake. As predicted and instructed by Guru Rinpoche, I offered Lhodrong Tulku the empowerments and transmissions of the treasures I had discovered up to that time. We were as happy as a reunited father and son. We both remembered our connection throughout many lives clearly enough to be able to compare recollections; our minds became as one.

"At Mount Kugyal I repaired the border-taming stupa that had been erected there by Guru Rinpoche. I saw signs that this would help the area as a whole and especially the dharma and welfare of the meditation colleges of upper Dokham. The deity Dokham Kugyal gave me a stupa of bell metal, four finger-widths in height.

"The next year, while I was traveling to gather grain in the town of Dzame Lingru, I met the Lord Refuge Lho Rinpoche. It was apparent that he was one of the Three Named Ratna, root inheritors of my treasures predicted in the treasure prophecies themselves. Because he was a monk I was initially unable to bring this up to him. However, he himself received indications to this effect from dakinis, and was encouraged by the treasure guardians. He bent down to my level, and I offered him the empowerments of *The Dakini Cycle* and the rest; the self-arisen stone image of Guru Rinpoche as a wealth deity that had been given to me above Lhasa by the Red Gongtsen Lightning Lasso; the six-eyed zi stone, worn by Guru Rinpoche, that I had found while opening the gate to Dalkyap, the sacred place in Surmang; and a portion of all the samaya substances in my possession.

"At Misty Fortress in Cham I met Kyodrak Salje. He was someone who did not accept anyone easily as a teacher. However, because of previous karma he observed signs of auspicious interdependence in relative truth, and said that he wanted the empowerments and transmissions for all of my treasures written down thus far. I offered him those, and also all of the samaya substances given me by the activity protector. This was in compliance with Guru Rinpoche's specific instructions.

"On my way back from the begging journey that winter I stayed in the upper floor of the Wenchung family home in Darong. I practiced, in retreat there, *The Dakini Cycle,* and was able to commit to writing the remainder of it. One night, the dakini Yeshe Tsogyal appeared to me in the costume of that region and said to me, 'The upper practice cave at Yangdzong Mountain of Fire was the site of two retreats performed by

Guru Rinpoche and his pure retinue, the lord and subjects. Each of these lasted for ten months. During the second one, the lord and subjects accepted disciples themselves. The site was blessed as the mandala of Vajraheruka, the embodiment of mind, and was used for that practice for seven generations. It is a particular residence of the empresses of the expanse, the wisdom dakinis. The rock to its left is the mandala of Vajrasattva. The mountain across from it is a residence of Hayagriva. There are many treasures concealed in that area by Guru Rinpoche. Among them is the representation of him called *Origin of All Siddhi;* it is in the practice cave at Yangdzong Mountain of Fire. Also in the cave are many teachings concerning *The Accomplishment of Guru Rinpoche's Mind.* Extract them.'

"Having received that indication and others, about five predictions in all, in the fourth month I read *The Padma Katang* and earnestly performed feasts and cleansing smoke offerings.[62] Guru Rinpoche appeared to me in the manner of a youthful atsara and repeated the previous predictions. He also instructed me that there needed to be a certain combination of persons and place for the treasures to be retrieved. After receiving his wondrous vajra dispensation, on the tenth day of the waxing phase of that month, I sent my son, Padma Tsewang; my ritual assistant, Mönlam; my attendant, Menlha; and my ganachakra companion of authentic family, Söga Wangmo, to Yangdzong to search for the treasures. They were persistent, and having reached the practice cave Padma Tsewang found the image.

"It was encased in a heart-shaped container of stone that was in the sand among the rocks inside the cave. The container was also packed with sand. Within it, along with the image, were white and blue scrolls of text, a few pieces of tree-bark inscribed with symbol script, and a large amount of samaya substance. They found all this without mishap, and it reached my hands safely.

"One night Guru Rinpoche appeared to me as an atsara adorned by the costume of a heruka, and predicted my discovery of treasures at Ludrak, Kalchen, and other places. The next day, I sent Dharmawardha to Dagyü Ludrak. He found the flesh of the brahmin Suryagarbha and some of Yeshe Tsogyal's hair. The door to the treasure opened of itself, and, amazed, he found the treasure in a hollow space within the rock.

"At the same time, the Five Forms of the Great King,[63] with a large retinue, appeared to my son Padma Tsewang in a dream and told him that if I did not quickly commit to writing the liturgy for their veneration that I had received, they would cause impediments for both me and my son. On the next day I wrote a short liturgy of offering.

"One night a well-dressed white man riding a white horse came to me, saying that he was from the deva realms. He said, 'I am Sönam Kundrup, 'Bringer of All Merit,' and I promise to guard the teachings of both you the Vidyadhara, and your son, for as long as they exist.'

"He had been my deva of birth in a previous life.[64] When I went to Jaryül I wrote a liturgy for his veneration.

"I then committed to writing *The Four Life Sadhanas* and

performed the approach and accomplishment of all of them, especially of *The Profound Life Sadhana.* Good signs of longevity arose.

"I sent my ritual assistant, Karma Mönlam, to Derge with a message for the Tulku Jamyang Khyentse Wangpo. On his journey, in Jitsatang, in front of the residence of its remarkable local deity, he found a thumb-sized zi stone, which he brought to me.

"In the previous Bird Year, Guru Rinpoche had appeared to me in the form of a yogin and predicted that in the Pig Year I would find some profound treasures concealed in the Protector Cave at the foot of Dagyü Kalchen Rock.[65] In the following Pig Year I was encouraged to retrieve the treasures by their protector, Nabun Genyen.[66] I mentioned all this to my disciple, Karma Döndam, and both he and his daughter, Ayu, dreamed of clear indications that I would discover treasure.

"So, accompanied by my son, Kunzang Dorje, and other disciples, I went to the Protector Cave at the foot of Kalchen Rock. Since it was the tenth day of the waning moon, we spent the day performing a hundred feasts, including the feast offering and fire offering of Padmadakini. After we had all become somewhat intoxicated by the feast liquor, we suddenly heard a thunderous crack, and, in the sight of twenty-five people, a lot of scrolls fell from the sky. These included *The Dakinis of the Expanse Cycle, The Four Sadhanas of Guru Rinpoche's Mind, The Black Hayagrivakilaya, The Vajrarishi Cycle,* and more—white scrolls, yellow scrolls, scrolls of Tibetan paper, symbol script written on bark, and scrolls written in Tibetan. When my assistant Karma Choksal was gathering these up, I told him drunkenly to throw those without legible symbols or other writing into the offering fire. Because the initial interdependence was correctly established, and through Guru Rinpoche's compassion, as soon as the smell of their burning reached my nose their words and meaning appeared vividly to me. This helped to quickly awaken my recollections.

"That night I went to sleep in the Cave of Power, which was beneath a rock like a Shivalingam, on the left of the main cave. In that cave, the treasure guardian, Nabun Genyen, gave me seven more scrolls. These included *Applications of the Guru's Mind Sadhanas; The General Instruction on Generation and Completion; The Sadhana of Ekajati, Rahula, and Vajrasadhu; The Wisdom Being; The Tamer of Beings;* and *The Sadhana of Mahadeva* with its applications.

"When I was a child, on my autumn begging route, the Red Gongtsen Lightning Lasso told me that there were pills of the five amritas to be found at Gongmar Chudil. However, because my tutor was so strict, I had no opportunity at that time to extract them.

"Much later, when I was almost sixty, I was again traveling to gather grain near Gongmar. Through the activity of Lightning Lasso, a roaring sound without physical cause began suddenly, throwing our horses and mules into panic. The treasure guardian displayed his own form and indicated slight displeasure at my delay in extracting the treasure. I reminded him of his samaya and he promised to present the treasure to me.

"At that time Guru Rinpoche prophesied,

'At conch-like Gongmar Chudil
Is my amrita of five families.'

"He also gave me other predictions at that time.

"After that, one night when I was in Lhasagong performing ceremonies for general welfare, I saw, in a mixture of meditation and dream, a blue man staring at me with glaring yellow eyes. He had a few people with him. He said to me, 'Tomorrow, go to the mountaintop where you can see the lake of Nabun Genyen. I will offer you a few things you need.'

"The next day I went up to the peak of the mountain there and offered a golden drink. I sent my companions to search the area, and fell asleep, exhausted by the climb. I was abruptly awakened by a loud crack that seemed to come from nowhere. Immediately after waking up, I saw, at the foot of the hill of rock called Horse-Nose, which is behind the mountain of Nabun Genyen itself, a white mist, like an unfurled bolt of silk, appear from the Dachu Lake. Within the mist was the treasure guardian Powerful Wisdom, in the form of a green snake emitting sparks of fire, filling the whole valley. After coming before me, he turned into the blue man I had seen the previous night and gave me pills that prolong life, consecrated by Guru Rinpoche at Samye and Yamalung; pills of nutritive essence created by the Worthy King Dza; and pills of medicine to dispel illness, created by the great rishis of medicine. Each of these was glistening with the dew of amrita. He also gave me a scroll of blue paper, saying, 'This is that text you needed.'

"Then he entered the mist from which he had appeared, and vanished.

"The scroll was *The Sadhana of the Wrathful Guru, the Tamer of the Haughty.*

"The next day I offered a feast and sent my son, Padma Tsewang; my ritual assistant, Mönlam; and my feast companion, Orgyen Tsetso, the daughter of Gyanye Döndam, to Kalchen Chudil. This was as instructed in the prophecies. They found white amrita pills of Vairochana, blue amrita pills of Akshobhya, yellow amrita pills of Ratnasambhava, red amrita pills of Amitabha, and green amrita pills of Amoghasiddhi. Because the extraction of these was a little delayed, the container of the pills had burst forth from its place of concealment. It appeared from the outside to be a mixture of earth and stone, and was the size of a child's fist.

"As soon as I received the pills, I ground them up and mixed them with other substances to increase the amount. While I did so, the village was filled with an amazingly delicious fragrance, which caused everyone to give rise to wonderment and trust.

"I then sent my disciple Karma Döndam to the practice cave of Mahahumkara at Kalchung Rock. In the rock to the cave's left were Guru Rinpoche's footprints. From that rock, Döndam extracted life-increasing substances of Vajrasattva consecrated by the master Mahahumkara. These consisted of a spoon-sized bundle of dharma medicine.

"I also sent my son, Padma Tsewang, and the other two whom I had sent to Chudil, to Medrak, where they found pills prepared by the dakini Yeshe Tsogyal through the transformation of a zombie into gold. At the same time Guru Rinpoche, appearing as a youthful monastic tantrika, explained to me the qualities of the sacred place of Medrak and instructed me that it was necessary to create a circumambulation path there. About thirty of us, followed by others, went there and presented elaborate cleansing smoke, golden drink, and feast offerings. I perceived the place as the palace of the Peaceful and Wrathful Sugatas, and wrote a guide to it on that basis.

"I then sent my son Padma Tsewang, my assistant Mönlam, and others to create a pathway to the place and, while doing so, to search for treasure. They found pills of White Manjushri, pills of Sarasvati, the materials for making an image, and other samaya substances—about ten types. That day about a hundred people were circumambulating the place. All of them saw rainbow clouds gathered at the peak and a rain of flowers, and heard the sound of the mantra of the Peaceful and Wrathful Ones issuing from Rulu Pass.

"After that I returned to Surmang Monastery. In my residence, Tashi Lhundrup Ling, I increased the amount of all the samaya substances I had received and then, filling two joined skull-cups with the amrita I had prepared in this way, I consecrated them through the solitary practice of a vira.[67] Everyone in the vicinity smelled a wondrous and delicious fragrance.

"I prepared supports, containing spirit-stones and yantras, for the protectors of the New and Old lineages, and for those of my own treasures in particular. I saw the protectors actually dissolve into the supports.

"When I went to gather dairy products, I passed a boulder containing an obstructive spirit at Mokpu Pass. I harassed the spirit by urinating fearlessly on his boulder. On the way back, I noticed my handprint in the rock, made when I had leaned on it while urinating.

"I then received the prediction of my discovery of treasure at Yangdzong. Yeshe Tsogyal told me that at Darong Mountain of Fire she had concealed a treasure which, like a flint stone that can produce fire in an instant, held the key to controlling the whole land. She said that if I extracted it, it could ensure the longevity of dharma in, and the stability of, all Tibet and especially the meditation colleges of upper Kham. However, I left it where it was, undecided as to its true benefit.

"That year, Guru Rinpoche instructed me in meditation and dreams about the need to combine the presence of certain persons in a certain place. Although my existing residence at Surmang was spacious, and my age made the establishment of a new residence very troublesome, I felt I should establish a retreat facility for the benefit of the teachings and beings, as he had instructed me. I searched for the eye of the land, and performed the taking of the ground.[68] After that, I was called by a messenger to the north, and there I went. While I was gone my son, Padma Tsewang, started to build a meditation hall. I performed *The Accomplishment of Prosperity of Excellent Jewel.* During it, all present saw, for as long as it takes to drink a cup of tea, a golden yellow light within the offerings. In the house of Chankyi Mingyur, I performed the same *Accomplishment of Prosperity.* A yellow DZAM syllable, as though written in gold, appeared of itself on the handle of the kila of meteoric iron that was among the practice supports.

"There was a prophecy that I should go at that time to Gatö Jowo to open the treasure door there, but circumstances made it difficult. I went to see the sacred place of Lhang Gyang in Jakok, and performed the same *Accomplishment of Prosperity* and also a cleansing smoke offering. Everyone in my camp saw a white rainbow cloud, like an unfurled bolt of silk, emerge from the peak. A rain of flowers fell from it. The Gatö Jowo image appeared to me and told me the story of Guru Rinpoche's concealment of profound treasure at its location. I received as siddhi a wonderful white calcite stone and a self-arisen stone stupa the size of a fist.

"When I was in Pelung and in the village of Dzeda the protector of Tago, the activity protector Atsara, appeared. Short and corpulent, with a topknot of conch and eyebrows and beard of turquoise, he was wearing both the robes of a monk and the costume of an atsara. He was seen every night by my attendant, Menlha, and others who were just outside my door. Every time he appeared, the whole house would shake. I ordered him to bring to accomplishment, without hindrance, my activity and that of my lineage. He told me many stories about his deeds in India and Tibet, starting with how he had been the custodian of the treasury of Vajrasana. He said that throughout my births in both India and Tibet, such as that as the great pandita Naropa, the keeper of the north gate of Nalanda, we had been connected through samaya. He was very affectionate, and taught me many beneficial mantras in the Prakrit language. Encouraged by my attendants, I wrote a liturgy for the presentation of offerings to him. Since that time, whether I am at home or traveling, he has accompanied me like my shadow, and whatever I think of is accomplished without hindrance. Because he is a wisdom deity in nature, he is gentle; because he has adopted the form of an activity protector, his activity is powerful and swift.

"On the night I reached Sumdo, the Secret of Body, a man wearing a white hat said to me, 'Tomorrow, while traveling, look around you. There is a reason.'

"The next morning, there was a great snowfall. On the day after, on our way, I found among the debris left by a departed group of nomads, in a patch of melted snow, a dark brown stone shaped like a tortoise. I was unsure whether it was the spirit-stone of Kugyal or a treasure vessel due to be opened in the future.

"I then easily reached the area below Darong Mountain of Fire. My son, Padma Tsewang, had more or less completed the building there. Relying as a companion upon Kalpingkabhadri, a woman of authentic family and a rebirth of Nanam Drongkyi, I decoded my treasure, *The Four Sadhanas of the Guru's Mind*, and wrote it out on paper. As I did so, the first copy of it was made by Karma Tendar, my nephew. When I began the decoding process, Guru Rinpoche, the Lake-Born Mahaguru, appeared to me surrounded by as many pure vidyadharas as there are stars in the sky. They blessed me with their three secrets. At that time I also reminded Ekajati, Rahula,

Vajrasadhu, and Dorje Yudrönma of their commitment to this teaching.

"I presented the cycle over time to its destined inheritors, such as the Lord Refuge Lho Rinpoche, proclaimed by Guru Rinpoche to be the emanation of Sokpo Lhapal; Matrul Rinpoche, Könchok Tendzin Chökyi Nyima, the emanation of the Madman of Bhutan; Jedrung Rinpoche, Trinlay Jampa Jungnay, the emanation of the victor Akshobhya; and Orgyen Nüden Dorje, the emanation of Nyangben Tingdzin Zangpo.

"The glorious Gyalwang Karmapa Khakhyap Dorje came to Nangchen at around the same time, and I encountered the mandala of his countenance. I offered him the image of Guru Rinpoche called *Fulfillment of All Wishes* that I had found at Yangdzong; a complete copy of *The Dakini Cycle;* the salt from the preservation of the remains of Ma Rinchen Chok that I had found at Rokpal Senge Namdzong; and portions of all the samaya substances I had found at Dalkyap, Medrak, and other places. Having heard of the image of Guru Rinpoche as the Vajradhara of Uddiyana that I had found at the spring in Lei, he asked for it, and I offered that as well. He kindly gave me the daily crown worn by both him and his predecessor; a letter of commendation, bearing his seal, written on yellow silk; and an aspiration for my longevity.

"At that time Taklung Ma Rinpoche, Tekchok Jigme Pawo, came to that area. He was one of the Three Named Ratna, the predicted root inheritors of my treasures; it was at that time that I first encountered his golden countenance. He told me that while he was living at the Shapdrung Residence at

Riwoche Monastery he had had a vision that I was undoubtedly a rebirth of Nupchen Sangye Yeshe. He therefore treated me with the utmost respect and veneration. At his request, I offered him the empowerments and transmissions for some of Chokgyur Lingpa's treasures. He was delighted, and made a hat that he said was a replica of the hat that Nupchen was wearing when he had seen him in the vision at his residence. He presented this to me to use as my ceremonial crown, and also presented me with many other fine things.

"On his way to gather grain in Dzagyü, he visited my retreat and residence. While there, he told me that he had received repeated prophecies indicating that he should receive my treasures, and therefore wished to do so. I offered him all the empowerments and transmissions of *The Great Bliss Dakini Cycle, The Four Mind Sadhanas,* and the rest. This was the excellent establishment of the interdependence commanded by Guru Rinpoche. At that time he told me to commit to writing *The Yamantaka All-Surpassing Mudra Cycle,* but because of its strictness, I delayed doing so. I offered him the skull-image that I had acquired, Nupchen's practice support; the vajra, Mahahumkara's practice support; the self-arisen image of the Four-Armed Mahakala on the skull of Prince Mune Tsenpo that I had discovered at Dalkyap; and a portion of every samaya substance in my possession.

"At the behest of the Lord Chingtu Rinpoche, in service to the well-being of all Tibet, Drongtrul Rinpoche—Orgyen Nüden Dorje—and I restored the eight stupas below Kalchen Rock that had been erected by Guru Rinpoche. While we were doing so, in the sight of Drongtrul Rinpoche and about thirty others, three scrolls concerning *The Mind Sadhanas* fell from the sky with a loud humming sound.

"I then invited him to my retreat. Because of the prophecy that he was to be an inheritor of my treasures, I offered him the empowerments and transmissions for all I had written out thus far—chiefly *The Dakini and Mind Sadhana Cycles*—and a portion of all the samaya substances. Since he told me that the undamaged heart of the bodhisattva Ever-Crying was destined to be a shrine object at the seat of the Drikung Kagyu, I sent it there.

"A messenger arrived from the capital of Nangchen, telling me that the King of Nangchen, a great bodhisattva, had passed into peace. I therefore made the requisite extensive funeral offerings. In service to his surviving family, I cast a torma of entrustment and liberation at Dzeno Pass. Its water-lord appeared in the form of a bright, white man with the lower body of a snake and accepted the offering.

"At around the same time I met Matrul Rinpoche, who was returning from Derge. He compiled a detailed list of the empowerments, transmissions, and texts of my treasures. Our meeting was like the reunion of a father and his son; because of his great affection for me, he cried at our parting and displayed an unwillingness to be separated from me.

"In the service of the Prince of Nangchen, I performed *The Secret Life Sadhana of the Mother* for a week. On the life-torma appeared a hair like a thread of light, four finger-widths in height, with life-essence appearing on its end like the orange stamens of a flower. Having seen indications of his great longevity in various meditation experiences and dreams, I offered him the life empowerment. At the same time, I offered him two images of Guru Rinpoche, with the aspiration that his possession of them would, through Guru Rinpoche's timely intercession, alleviate the border conflicts with China. One of these images was of porcelain and showed Guru Rinpoche seated in the Maitreya posture, like the deities of China. It had been found in the practice cave of Mahahumkara at Kalchen Rock by my son, Padma Tsewang; my assistant, Karma Mönlam; and my companion at the ganachakra in the Protector Cave at Dzagyü, Rongchungza Drölkar, a rebirth of Shelkar Dorje Tso whom I had sent there in search of treasure. The other image, also received by them as siddhi in the same place, was of Guru Rinpoche in the form of a wealth-deity, seated on a lion. Together with the presentation of these, I performed for the Prince *The Accomplishment of Prosperity of Excellent Jewel.*

"I had received Guru Rinpoche's command to go south in the Dragon Year.[69] I therefore went to Riwoche in that year. I met Jedrung Rinpoche, Trinlay Jampa Jungnay, the emanation of the victor Akshobhya and one of the Three Named Ratna. He had seen clear indications that he should receive my treasures. I offered him all that had been thus far written out; the interdependence was excellent. I also offered him the image of Guru Rinpoche made of naga clay that I had found at Samye Yamalung; the wish-fulfilling jewel spirit-stone of the naga king Madro Zichen, the size of a kite's egg, that I had found on the riverbank below Samye; and most of the jewels and a portion of all the samaya substances I had discovered as treasure. When he examined the jewel that had been given to me by the four great nyens and held it in his hands, it gave forth a stream of melted butter. He placed it at his pillow and venerated it for a month. As a result, he found thirteen measures of gold that had been concealed by his predecessor.

"One morning, while we were staying in Tsewang Gatsal at Yangön Monastery, I and all the monks attending me saw the deva general Yikgyal appear in the form of a child. He gave me some of the dakini Yeshe Tsogyal's red bodhichitta; it looked like a red calcite stone.

"I offered the mahasiddha Lama Rikdzin some empowerments and transmissions from my treasures, and the profound instructions of the Great Perfection.

"When I went to Zegyal, I discovered in the Valley of Varahi a stream of what looked like blood that continued to flow for seven days. At the same time there fell a rain of five-colored crystal flowers, plentiful enough that one could gather handfuls of them. At the Pass of Hayagriva, I saw a joy swirl, turning to the left, in the clouds.[70]

"I did a retreat at White Lake Hermitage, performing *The Life Sadhana* in the service of Gochen Lama Tsewang Tendzin. One night a brown man with blonde hair and beard appeared and said, 'What you want has been placed here.' Then he touched the lakeshore and vanished. The next day I found placed there, between covers of stone shaped like the blade of a kila, a few sheets of paper and a few yellow scrolls. These were *The Subtle Drop Vajrasattva Cycle* and *Tsogyal's Collar Pouch.*

"It also became clear to me that there was a treasure in a rock shaped like a life-vase across the lake. I secretly sent my assistant, Karma Mönlam, and my companion for *The Life Sadhana,* Tseyang, a niece of the Dakini of Doshul. When they got to the lakeshore, my assistant became intoxicated, as though with liquor, by Guru Rinpoche's compassion. Exhilarated, he tore off his clothes and ran naked into the lake. In places it came up to his armpits and in other places just to his waist. He reached the rock and found the door to the treasure. Picking at the rock, he found that some of the stones were loose. As soon as he removed them, the whole area became filled with a fine fragrance. Concealed within the rock were life substances of Vajrasattva, pills of Vajrasattva vase water, and some of Namkhai Nyingpo's clothing. On his way back across the lake, he spilled a spoonful of the powdered substances into the lake. Instantly, the whole lake changed color and became fragrant. Because his previous exhilaration had dissipated, he was somewhat frightened on the way back, but made it across safely.

"In the early morning of the seventh day of my retreat, I heard the words, 'Lama Tsewang will live for twenty years.'

"I perceived the whole area of Ze as a crystal stupa blessed by the wisdom of the seven tathagathas, its foundation resting on the golden ground at the world's bottom, and its apex reaching the formless realms.[71] I therefore offered feasts and made repeated aspirations.

"While performing *The Descent of Blessing for Sacred Places* at Gochen Retreat, I perceived the place purely as the realm of

Heruka, and each of the representations as the three roots in tiers, surrounded by viras and dakinis as numerous as the sesame seeds that spill from an opened pod.

"When I went to Pen Retreat, I perceived the two clay hills in front of it as a white deva protector and a blue naga protector, both wearing armor. When I enlisted the service of the local deities there, all the other ones appeared and took samaya.

"When I was performing service for Trawotang, from the rock across the valley appeared a wild tsen in armor and from the lower valley a teurang in the form of a child riding a goat, with a yellow nyen riding a sheep behind him, and other spirits. I gave them all rules to follow.[72]

"At Gyalchen Retreat I gave Lama Tashi *The Vitality Entrustment of the Dakinis* from the treasure of Chöje Lingpa. I clearly saw the dakinis of the five families. There was also indication of their resentment of the large number of disciples to whom I was giving the empowerment.

"While performing a public empowerment in Shelnang, a flashing white light appeared from the east. I sent a few people to investigate. One of them found a large, oblong rock covered with emblems of body, speech, and mind. They built a throne of stone and placed the rock on top of it.

"In Gurulung I saw the deva general Yikgyal, brilliant white and wearing the costume of a king; he seemed inseparable from the mountain there that is his residence.

"While I was performing *The Pill Consecration of the Wrathful Guru* at Yangön Ladrang, I saw the Wrathful Guru, indivisible from the substances being consecrated, with the garland of his mantra revolving continuously in his heart. I also heard the mantra's sound.

"Around the same time, Jedrung Rinpoche placed the flower of his command on my head concerning the need to commit to writing the whole *Vajrarishi Cycle*, which had been concealed in parts in various places, such as the sacred place Kalchen. To serve as the interdependent equivalent of a companion, he gave me an image of Vajradakini made of dzimkshim metal.

"Previously, after the Terchen's passing, I had performed *The Sadhana of the Rishi Loktripala*, and its controlling, burning, and casting, in the service of his consort and children. At that time, I committed to writing a brief daily liturgy that came to me as a mind treasure. However, because the rest of it was so strict, I left it unwritten.

"Now, at this time, I committed to writing on paper the cycle's major tantras, as commanded by the noble guru. The rishi Stainless Virtue, wearing a white robe and holding a mala of conch, surrounded by as many truth-accomplishing rishis—both wisdom and mundane—as the stars in the sky, appeared to me several times. The signs of blessing were good.

"When Lama Rikdzin and I led *The Amrita Accomplishment of the Assembly of the Guru's Wisdom* above the Drukpakang, I saw on several occasions the deities above the amrita, heard the sound of the mantras issuing from their mouths, and, in the sky above, saw the victors of the five families and their realms.

"In the Temple of Sargang, I saw Vajrasadhu, the dark red blacksmith.

"In the past, the deva general Yikgyal had prophesied to me of the need for me to go to the sacred place of Pomne, the treasures of which were under his protection. At this time, the quick-acting mara-tsen Rakne appeared to me as a monk riding a black horse and said to me, 'You really must come soon.'

"So I went to Pomne. At Tsukpu Dewachenpo I performed a ganachakra, accompanied by my feast companion, Tsedzin Lhamo, and about thirty disciples. I sent my son, Padma Tsewang; my ritual assistant, Karma Mönlam; my attendant, Menlha; and others to search for the treasure. To the right of the lower cave's doorway they found *The Shvana Cycle*.[73] The yellow scrolls were contained in a sealed wooden casket the size of a finger, similar to sandalwood and covered with earth and stone. They also found, in the same location, *The Trikaya Supplication,* which was written on red silk. To the left of the middle cave's doorway was a protruding hollow rock, sealed with stone. When the seal was removed, the area became filled with the fragrance of medicinal herbs. Inside the rock were instructions on medicine. All of this was brought to me.

"I then returned to Darong and went to and fro in the area fulfilling the wishes of various patrons. While I was at Rachung Padma Tsang, some newly formed clay fell from the rock surface of the local deity's mountain. Where the clay had been, I found the sword that had protected Nupchen called 'Enemies'

Doom.' It was through the activity of the treasure guardian Yamuntri that it reached me.

"When I reached the area of my home, I saw signs that there was a treasure at Yerong Rock, which resembled a white conch shell. On the tenth day of the month, after performing a feast offering to Guru Rinpoche, I sent my assistant, Mönlam; my feast companion of authentic family, Söga Wangmo; and three others—altogether a group of five monastics and laypersons—to search. Söga Wangmo found a hollow piece of weathered wood, larger than a fist, and a seashell. When the wood was cut open, it was revealed to be white sandalwood. Inside it were the yellow scrolls of *The Lower Activity of Vajrakila,* two finger-breadths in height.

"Some time after that Karma Chökyong, a monk of Kyodrak Monastery, earnestly encouraged me to commit to writing the Vajrakila teachings I had found. I therefore set down on paper *The Upper Activity*. One night during this time, while in a state combining meditation experience and luminosity, I found myself in a place that appeared to be the meteoric iron peak of Mount Malaya. I was transformed into the Lord of Secrets, Vajrapani. Surrounded by the Five Destined Ones and others, I taught a sadhana and many instructions conforming to *The Fragment of the Vajrakila Root Tantra.* Members of the assembly wrote these down on sheets of gold with ink of liquid vaidurya. The moment I awoke, all of the meaning of the yellow scrolls I had found appeared in my mind without any impediment. In the company of my companion, Nigupta Kalpibhadra, I wrote it all out. In the treasure upheaval that occurred while I was writing out *The Shvana Cycle*, a few of my monks got into a loud argument. As that would indicate, the words that emerged were sharp and clear, and the activity of the cycle proved to be extremely efficient. At night, my room was filled with firelight and flashes of lightning. Among the shooting sparks of fire, I saw on several occasions the samaya-bound Kila Guardians.

"Accompanying the Lord Refuge Lho Rinpoche, at Gongmarshöl I convened a Great Accomplishment Assembly of *The Guru's Mind Sadhana* from my treasures. At first there occurred the mischief of spirits, such as earthquakes and so on. The disturbances gradually ended and the spirits stopped coming around.

"I invited Lho Rinpoche to my retreat, where we convened a Great Accomplishment Assembly of *The Dakini Cycle* from my treasures. During it I saw the deities and heard the mantra.

"He told me that he wanted additional important treasure articles, so I offered him the bone of Prince Mune Tsenpo bearing self-arisen images and a relic of the Buddha Korwajik that was the size of a large bird's egg.

"In the distant past, the ashes of the Buddha Korwajik had been cast into the ocean. They were swallowed by a large fish, whose body became a mass of relic pills. Later, the siddha and master Luyipa, having arisen from his all-pervasive samadhi, found the body of the fish and brought it to Jambudvipa so that it could be a support for faith. Through Guru Rinpoche's compassion, it was given to me by the protector Red Tsiu. This was the relic I offered Lho Rinpoche.

"It had been predicted that the Three Named Ratna, of whom Lho Rinpoche was one, and Drongyül Rinpoche were to be the principal inheritors of my treasures. Through the excellent interdependence of this, they always asked me for the dharma and substance treasures that were theirs by right without my ever having to tell them of their existence. This was due to the activity of Guru Rinpoche, the Lake-Born.

"Lho Rinpoche and his disciples convened a Great Accomplishment Assembly of *Tukdrup Barchay Kunsel*, the treasure of Chokgyur Lingpa, in front of Danyin Kalarongo, where it had been found. A female spirit appeared to him, coming from Datö. She had sores on her scalp and was surrounded by seven ghosts and spirits. She was harming the whole region, and wishing to impede his activity caused a violent wind to strike his tent. He knew what was happening and asked me to intervene. I compelled her with the samadhi of Manjushri Yamantaka; she appeared before me and offered me her life-essence, which I accepted.

"Previous to this, while performing a ganachakra in the Protector Cave at Kalchen Rock, I had sent my son, Padma Tsewang, and my assistant, Mönlam, to search for treasure at Kalchen. In the practice cave of Mahahumkara they had found an image of Guru Rinpoche as the god of wealth, riding a lion. Lho Rinpoche now asked me for this image, which I offered to him.

"I then went to gather grain in Chamshi and nearby. Taklung Matrul Rinpoche knew that there was a treasure concealed on his family's property in Dzongtsa and asked me to retrieve it. I felt that it should be left where it was, with a stone marker built on top of it. However, he insisted, so, with a few disciples, I went into his fields and found a mongoose made of black stone, images of both Black Jambhala and Vaishravana, and the spirit-stone of an upasaka protector. I gave these to his family.

"In the neighboring village, Lho Rinpoche performed a divination, and as a result instructed me to set up a representation of the local deity. One night, while I was engaged in this, the local deity, the Upasaka of Nabun, appeared to me in the form of a human chieftain and said, 'I have always abided by Guru Rinpoche's commands and samaya. However, my daughter has recently taken up with a ghost, and under his influence is becoming unhappy. Could you help?'

"On the next day, I dispatched ransom offerings and repeatedly presented singed offerings.

"The Gyalwang Karmapa was traveling in Kham and had camped at Chitak. I went to meet him and offered him an image of Guru Rinpoche that I had made from materials I had found at Medrak, the sword of Nupchen called 'Enemies Doom,' and a copy of *The Four Sadhanas of the Guru's Mind.* He was pleased.

"When I went to Lhokok, I performed a ceremony in the service of the teachings and well-being of Gochen Retreat. When I sprinkled the monastery with banishing substances, I saw many spirits, and what appeared to be white and black dogs, run off to another region, making a tremendous noise. After completing the kila prevention and control ceremonies,

I performed a fire offering. During it, the great wrathful gingkaras emerged from the flames and filled the room and surrounding area.[74]

"When I was performing service to the region of Putok, the gods and spirits of that area came before me like an army and promised to accomplish activity.

"When I offered ablution to the Drerong Mutri Temple, I perceived it as the palace of Amitayus.

"Because of a vision, I sent my assistant, Karma Mönlam, to Doshul Beacon Rock. On the face of it was a flat stone the size of a yak's load pad. He removed it, and discovered a brown stone chest.

"I perceived Four Dog Fortress as the equivalent of Akanishtha Blazing Mountains of Fire, and as the realm of Great Splendor Vajrakumara.[75] The Kila Guardians, the male and female Shvanas, appeared in the form of dogs barking violently. I wrote a guide to the place based on my pure perception.

"An old man wearing armor approached me, saying he was the ruler of the area, and pointed out a sharp white rock above the fortress with a white boulder like a monument on top of it. He told me that it marked the site of the cremation of Kuje Sengchen, and was built according to the Bön tradition.

"At Ngonegar the Four Ladies, the other Kila Guardians, and the tsens and upasakas of the area appeared in their own forms. I reminded them of their commitment.

"When I placed *The Yantra Proclaiming Samaya to All Gods and Spirits* on the peak of Kangyal Mukmo, I saw that all the gods and spirits from Mukmo all the way to Dilyak took the samaya vow.

"One night while I was in Sunang performing service to the region, the people in my encampment were sitting around telling stories. I had been asleep, but awoke with the impression that a burglar had entered the encampment. I sent someone to look; he found the burglar, who ran away, among the horses and mules.

"While I was at Tami Retreat, in front of the representation of the Drala of Drong, I saw him as a short monk, and wrote a liturgy for his veneration. It appeared to me that uphill from that place was a practice cave used by both the learned Vairochana and his disciple Yudra Nyingpo, but I was unable to go look.

"While at Blue Cave Retreat, I became certain that the Dakini of Saza was the rebirth of Chöku Orgyan Butri, the consort of Taksham Nüden Dorje.[76] I therefore established both physical and mental connection with her. While I was there, from the place's self-arisen bhaga, the sacred residence of Vajravarahi, a stream of red fluid like bodhichitta began to flow. The Dakini of Saza told me that she had heard that this had happened when Taksham had been there, but that, aside from that, she had never seen such a thing. Although the area was very dry, water began to flow in the streams. The dakini addressed her niece and others, saying, 'Even if you just consider the sudden flow of water in this dry place, it is certain that the qualities of this lama are inconceivable. I am too old to do so, but if one of you young women were to bear a child of his family line and establish a branch of it here, it would bless and help this area tremendously.'

"She was quite insistent about this, but it didn't happen.

"I consecrated the temple at Kangnang. While doing so, I saw many forms of deities, too indistinct to name, emerge from the sky behind the hill to the temple's right and dissolve into the temple itself.

"While I was at Palme Monastery in Gam, I met a life-long retreatant, a former teacher there, whom I recognized to be the rebirth of one of Marpa the Translator's disciples.

"I performed a public empowerment at Gyalchen Monastery. In the crowd I saw a female spirit wearing a ragged blue blanket, running around and looking at the people. I compelled her with visualization, and she fled. She harmed one of the horses of the monastery's smaller residence.

"While I was at Lhatse Retreat an old man who called himself Ahumtsang approached me leading a little boy by the hand. As soon as I saw him, I realized that the boy was the rebirth of Putsang Gyurme, my companion's deceased brother. I gave them three fine porcelain cups.

"The treasure guardian of Pomne appeared to me one night as a white man riding a white horse and gave me a round brown stone, which he said was a jewel. The next day, Lama Chetruk's son actually gave me a round brown stone with a design like an eye. I felt that it was the spirit-stone of the local deity.

"At Riwoche Retreat, its local deity appeared in Chinese dress and promised to accomplish activity. One night while staying at the New College at Riwoche, I saw Sangye Wön, the dharmakaya itself.[77] This later turned out to be an indication that I would acquire a representation of him. While I was there, an old monk showed up each night, displaying a variety of moods. I think he was the guardian of the monastery's wealth. One night, during the time when I was offering the empowerments and transmissions of the Oral Lineage of Surmang to the lamas of Riwoche, I dreamed that five women each gave me a garland of flowers.

"When I convened a Great Accomplishment Assembly of Vajraheruka and Vajrakila at Agyatsang, and while I was reciting *The Exhortation of the Vidyadharas*, the entire mandala of the Vidyadhara Guru appeared to my pure perception. During that time many spirits, such as a spirit-king with the appearance of a ragged monk, moved to other areas.

"When I performed *The Accomplishment of Prosperity* at Kyuratsang, I saw that a malevolent naga living at the base of a boulder on the bank of the Ngema River had enslaved many of the region's spirits. I compelled him, and I think things improved somewhat.

"When I reached Sharda in Nangchen, the road was blocked and a sudden hailstorm began. I pointed at it with the threatening gesture, and the storm went elsewhere.

"A messenger was sent from Kyodrak to summon me. On the way, in Kamda, a tsen living in a house on top of Lower Lharu Rock, offended by my presence, attacked me. He was assisted by a female spirit from Dzadü. They succeeded in making my horse lie down. I dispatched a ransom offering and compelled them through samadhi, and they promised never to harm me again.

"The previous summer, while begging, I had stayed one night at Goche. I dreamed that in a tent made from the skin of animals with poles made from their ribs and pegs made from their horns were living a lot of rakshasis. In the tent's doorway, I entered the pride of being the Mighty Hayagriva and compelled them. In the voices of spirits, they offered their life-essence mantras and promised never to harm anyone carrying those mantras in writing. I committed to writing their promise as a contract.

"I went to Kyodrak Camp and performed a Vajrakila fire offering, during which Vajrakumara and his retinue of deities appeared within the fire and accepted the offerings. When the fire was extinguished, there were indications that the power of the mischievous spirits of the locality was diminished. I performed *The Controlling Malevolent Spirits Ritual;* as a result many spirits with their armies of ghosts went elsewhere. I offered the three tulkus of Kyodrak together with many lamas and monks the empowerments and transmissions of all my treasures and especially of *The Great Life-Kila of Existence and Tranquility,* as predicted by Guru Rinpoche. I also committed to writing *The Vital Essence Entrustment of the Shvanas* there and offered them that as well. While I did so, the guardians displayed their own forms; signs of their accomplishment of activity arose. In the service of the tulkus and lamas, I performed *The Secret Life Sadhana of the Mother* in retreat at Sun Moon Cave. One early morning during that retreat, I saw the father and mother life deities in the midst of a mass of light in the center of the mandala. I expressed the wish to collect from the vases in their hands the life-essence of samsara and nirvana; amrita flowed from their vases into the life-support substances. In that and other ways, there were indications that the tulkus and lamas would live long.

"During the same period, the local upasaka guardian displayed his true form to me, and complained that the misconduct of the local people—chiefly lack of hygiene, responsibility, and fidelity—had contaminated his health, and that the growing influence of water spirits was making it uncomfortable for him to remain in the area. He was ready to leave. To help him, I wrote a liturgy for reminding the upasaka naga of his pledge, concealed a naga vase next to the lake at Khyungtra Cave, and so on; this helped the teachings and welfare of the area.

"In the service of Lana, I built an Ill-Fortune Subduing Stupa there, imprisoning spirits of corrupt samaya beneath its foundation. Several signs that these spirits had been summoned and caught arose in my meditation experience and dreams. In particular, on the day of the stupa's consecration, a rain of five-colored wisdom stupas fell and dissolved into it.

"At Nyingtangshung I performed a cleansing smoke offering ceremony in service to that area. That morning, in the mist that had arisen, I saw many of the local deities, appearing as men in armor, led by Dzagyal.

"One night while I was staying in the upper story of the Lamas' Residence at Kyodrak, I heard a loud bang from the roof. At the same time the building shook. Everyone outside heard a loud bang that seemed to be coming through my window from inside the building. The next morning, I asked the custodian, Jamyang, to look on the roof. He found a round stone box. It was a dharma treasure given to me by the upasaka. The round, marked stone that I had received at the peak above Kagyu Latso also turned out to be a container.

"At Drije Hortsang I saw the spirit-king of that area.

"When I performed ceremonies in the service of the region of Dochu, at Chaptigya, all the deities of that region appeared, displaying their pleasure. When I performed *The Summoning and Controlling of Enemies,* I saw a purple wolf dissolve into the support. I also saw that a few people were under the control of the area's elementals. When I subsequently performed *The Control of Enemies* at Nagong Chöka, I saw a large army of devas, nagas, and nyens.

"One night while I was traveling to gather grain in Dagyü, I saw that someone with magical power to the west was summoning an elemental with the form of a corpulent monk. The spirit was traveling on the Dachu River.

"When I got home, my disciple, the great yogin Lama Padma Trime Loden, presented me with a fine and extensive mandala offering, and for an entire month encouraged me to commit to writing *The Manjushri Yamantaka Cycle* retrieved from Kacho Rock. I then placed atop my head the flower of command that I had already received from Taklung Matrul Rinpoche, Tekchok Jigme Pawo; Jedrung Rinpoche, Trinlay Jampa Jungnay; and many other holy beings. Because this cycle, *Manjushri the All-Surpassing Mudra*, is so strict, I had kept it secret for eighteen years. By this time, however, the people and teachings of Tibet began to be threatened by the malevolent intentions and deeds of barbarians, and there was no way to know what was going to happen. I couldn't just do nothing. So I ignored the possible risk to myself, and one-pointedly prayed to Guru Rinpoche, father and mother, for permission to write it out. Once I received their command and assurance that the time was right, I convened a feast assembly including as companions, for the sake of discernment, Kachö Wangmo and Kalzang Drönma. I began to carefully commit to writing on paper what I correctly decoded from the dakinis' symbol script. Throughout the time it took me to do this, the dakini Yeshe Tsogyal was present in the form of a Tibetan woman wearing a stainless white woolen robe. I also saw in pure perception that Ekajati, the Guardian of Mantra, was there day and night in the form of a human woman.

"When I had difficulty decoding some of the words, a woman named Buga, a patron who had found a treasure box shaped like a tortoise shell containing Yamantaka teachings, dreamed that she should give this to me. She did, and I was able to decode the remainder of the treasure without impediment.

"During this, Padma Trime Loden, who had encouraged me to

decode the cycle, saw the door to my room open of itself every night and a mass of fire bright enough to illuminate an area a mile wide pass into my room. He also saw, several times, a short but well-proportioned woman wearing lots of fine jewelry standing by my window, her body shining so brightly that its light could fill the whole region.

"What he was seeing was the arrival of the great protector Rahula and the presence of Ekajati, both of whom are guardians of that treasure.

"The scribe who was the first to ever commit the treasure to writing was Padma Trime Loden himself. He was not only my disciple and a great yogin, but had been connected to me throughout many lives, such as when he had been born as Lharje Rokchen.

"Once it was completed, I first presented the ripening empowerments to seven people, including my son Padma Tsewang Dechen Chokdrup, the realized Trime Loden, and five other worthy disciples. During the ceremony, the deities appeared above each of the empowerment implements, and other signs of blessing arose. When I gave *The Entrustment of Ekajati,* tiny hearts appeared amidst what seemed to be bright red blood within the amrita contained in a skull-cup, which served as the representation of her vital essence. This is a sign of blessing described in the text itself.

"We then performed a week of Yamantaka practice in the service of the teachings and general welfare of Tibet, including a torma reversal. Clear signs of successful protection and reversal arose. I feel that our practice assisted in the gradual pacification of the conflict that was occurring at the time. During the practice, I saw the deities, received predictions from them, and at times smelled perfume and sometimes blood.

"After that my son Padma Tsewang performed the approach and accomplishment. Others heard the sound of a roaring bull coming from underground, beneath his residence. He also found out by accident that if he pointed his forefinger at bees or other insects while reciting the eighty-syllable mantra, they became paralyzed.

"The realized Trime Loden performed the approach and accomplishment three times. While he was doing so, sparks flew about his room, his cabin shook, and other remarkable external and internal signs appeared. An indication of his magical power is that when some rats knocked over his offering torma and he clapped his hands to scare them off, two of the rats dropped dead on the spot. When he blew at a hailstorm, the hailstones caught fire.

"I went to Drupgar in the north and performed service to the lamas and monks there. During this, and when I dispatched the ransom offering, many of the area's malevolent male and female spirits appeared.

"I convened a Great Accomplishment Assembly of Vajrakila; during it I saw Vajrakumara. During the invitation of the protector Lekden Mahakala, I experienced in pure perception the actual arrival of Mahakala, the single father of all protectors, surrounded by a hundred thousand deva warriors. Yudrak

Tulku was the regent of the assembly. During one of the later sessions he discovered a tiny heart stuck to his shoulder; this was a sign of the accomplishment of Ekajati. When we received empowerment during the reception of siddhi, numerous deities emanated from the deities of the mandala and dissolved into me. We concluded the practice with the casting of torma. When the great torma was cast, signs of the prevention of invasion arose.

"Mipam Rinpoche, the lord of the learned, came there and I met him. I had the honor of offering him service through both empowerment and ceremonies for his well-being. He was extremely generous to me both in the material way and in his unlimited trust in me. As requested in a letter from the chieftain Orgyen Norbu, I performed the protection and reversal rituals of Yamantaka in service to Mipam Rinpoche. During them, I saw signs that the mischief of spirit-kings and strong curses directed at him were turned away. I also cast a protection circle around him that was created using the same cycle.

"When I convened a Great Accomplishment Assembly of *The Guru's Mind Sadhanas* from my own treasures at Yangshar Monastery, I saw above the mandala Guru Rinpoche in the form of Uddiyana Vajradhara, father and mother, wearing the sambhogakaya costume. On the fourth day a finger-wide, three-jointed stalk of fresh Indian durva grass, the most auspicious substance connected with longevity, appeared on my table. It was a definite sign that I would live long. When we finished the accomplishment activity with its torma-casting and reversal, a fierce thunder and hailstorm occurred, an extremely good sign in the context of direct action. On the day

I performed a public empowerment, both the self-generation and front-generation deities appeared vividly, bestowing blessings. I appealed to the dakini Singhamukha for her intervention in the matter of the lawsuit between Drupgar and Tridu, and while doing so I saw her. I also presented offerings and veneration to Ekajati, Achi, the activity protector Atsara, and other guardians of the teachings; signs of their intervention arose, and the suit was settled amicably. As a result, people in both China and Tibet were pleased with me.

"I went again to Drupgar and convened an Accomplishment Assembly of Vajrakila. I saw various things in accord with the generation stage of that practice. Because someone in my home region was energetically cursing me, Könchok Tsering and I performed the ceremony for reversing such things; signs that the curse was reversed arose.

"A daughter of the Tseza family had died under unfortunate circumstances. I engaged in virtue on her behalf and came to feel that her eventual human rebirth was assured.

"At Tashi Gang I consecrated the Mara-Subduing Stupa there. While doing this, I saw many wisdom stupas dissolve into it. When I performed a feast offering in the same place, I saw for a long time a young lama wearing monastic robes and a meditation hat, with a yogin wearing a white cotton robe and cotton hat behind him. These were Drikung Chung Rinpoche and Rechung Dorje Drakpa.

"One day, in the mountains near Tridu, I saw both White and Green Tara.

"When I convened an Amrita Accomplishment Assembly at Drupgyü Monastery, even though it was wintertime, by the fourth day the inside and outside of the monastery were filled with the fragrance of the amrita. I saw many deities of the three roots, such as the nine vidyadharas, in a tent of five-colored light above the mandala.[78] Others saw remarkable things such as smoke and sparks coming from the amrita vessel. When we opened it, the amrita blazed with blue light, and the larger pieces bore the images of deities, so distinct that all who saw them were certain as to their identity.

"When I was performing service to Nyindzongla Monastery, it appeared to me that the basis of a curse afflicting the monastery was buried beneath its kitchen, but it would have been difficult to dig up. In that region there is only one spring; there is therefore concern that it might dry up. I presented offerings to the nagas there, and the flow of water increased.

"At Yudrak, at the behest of its lamas, the father and the mother, I convened an Amrita Accomplishment Assembly using *The Vajrakila Cycle* and, the year after, *The Wrathful Vidyadhara Cycle.* During these, I saw innumerable deities—peaceful, passionate, and wrathful—adorned with the marks and signs, and of uncertain appearance. There are no accounts of anyone performing an Amrita Accomplishment in that area before that. Because some of the local deities are spiteful, such as the one from Sedrong Mountain, I was unsure how successful the practice would be. However, it went very well both times. During these assemblies, many of the benevolent local deities, such as Gyokchen Dongray, took human form and attended the gatherings, reciting the mantras melodiously.

"Yutrul Rinpoche's consort Sukhadhari, who bore the marks of a wisdom dakini, asked me repeatedly to sing spontaneously of my experiences at that time. I sang the following song, an account of my experiences and visions:

"Lord gurus and deities, omniscient of the three times—
I pray to you with devotion's yearning.

"The various evils of these dregs of time sadden me.
Yet through the compassion of my kind gurus, my refuge,
And through the blessing of the Lord Padmasambhava,
We have assembled here in order to gather the
accumulations and purify obscurations.

"This is one of Tibet's twenty-five sacred places.
At the foot of Yudrak, the sacred site of Kyura,
This temple contains the three jewels.
The tulku vajra-holder is the leader of the yogins.
His consort is Sukha, so generous with all she has.
These two brought together the food, funds, and place.
Last year, that of the ox, I and seven tulkus and lamas[79]
With more than a hundred and fifty male and female
monastics and laypersons
Performed a Vajrakila Great Accomplishment,
And this year the Amrita Accomplishment of
The Guru And The Eight Dispensations.

"During these, in visions combining meditation and dream,
I have been accepted by Shriheruka.
The glory of summer has flourished here.
The matrikas and dakinis have gathered like clouds.

Flowers signifying excellence have fallen like rain.
All the dakinis, those with bodies and those without,
Have joined the birds in the sky above.
I have heard the mantras sung by the dakinis of space.
I have heard the secret language of the viras of the
five families
Buzzing like bees,
And have seen their playful dance of spontaneous
appearances.

"What we have done here has meaning.
We have accomplished the happiness of beings
in this place.
We have served the secret mantra teachings.
This old man goes from place to place;
Here I have done something genuinely great.

"In answer to the request of the consort,
Sukhadhari,
I, Dechen Barway Dorje, offer this.
May all of you—father, mother, and children—
Live long and benefit beings.

"As this was in the third month, the ice on the Drichu River was melting. I was told that if we did not leave soon, we might not be able to cross it. I entrusted this matter to the upasaka protector Dorje Nordzin. On the day we camped at the river's bank, it was shallow where we were, allowing us an easily crossed ford in any case. On the next morning a little snow fell, and we easily crossed the river on top of the snow and ice. When we reached the other side, we heard the ice start to crack.

This was a sign of the accomplishment of activity.

"Bearing the considerable offerings I had received, we returned to my retreat. Once I was home, all of the more thoughtful people of the area petitioned me to build a monastery, as I had been commanded by the victorious fathers and sons.

"I had spent my youth in the impartial service, to the best of my ability, of the teachings and beings, and I had been content with whatever I had. By this time I was at the age where one has no wish or plan beyond awaiting death. However, according to Guru Rinpoche's prediction, if a monastery were established there it would help the teachings and beings in general and especially prevent instability affecting the teachings and welfare of the region. I took that to heart and in obedience to the command of the victorious fathers and sons, and in order to fulfill the hopes of patrons and the people of the area, we began digging the foundation of a twenty-pillared monastery with a gatehouse. We started on the third day of the month Saga in the Male Wood Tiger Year, the year of the fifteenth cycle called 'Virtuous.'[80] On that day I offered cleansing smoke and golden drinks, entrusting activity to all the resident virtuous spirits. Nabun the Upasaka, Dzagyal Mokshe, and others promised to guard the monastery for the duration of its existence, and said that they would assist us in every way, down to carrying earth and stone. They seemed extremely pleased. I spoke to them of our needs, and when the digging began, we found an abundance of stones suitable for the building. People called it 'stone treasure;' it was certainly an answer to our prayers.

"While examining the ground for nagas, I saw the indistinct

forms of the eight nagas as well as many deva and naga children playing among the clouds. On that day, the clouds cast their first flowers, making the soil dark brown and soft. At the same time, we first heard the loud drum of summer resounding in all directions. The environmental signs were good from the start. I therefore feel that if the lamas and monks of future generations at this monastery are whole-heartedly concerned with the care of the teachings, we can hope for benefit to the teachings and beings. My intention in building it was slightly different from that of those who, because they wish to be lamas, search for property and, once they acquire it, call it a monastery. My confidence in the great benefit this monastery will bring to the teachings and beings in general and especially to this lineage and to the people of this area is drawn from the infallible words of Guru Rinpoche, who is omniscient of the three times.

"At this time my disciples Kagyu Tashi, Yunying Özer, and two others—four friends—came from Kyodrak. Previously, while he was in the retreat at Kyodrak, Kagyu Tashi had been told by Tashi Chöpel, the learned and accomplished lama from the Palpung Retreat, that when Jamgön Lodrö Taye was compiling *The Treasury of Instructions* he had remarked, 'Although the Barom Kagyu is one of the four primary divisions of the Kagyu, its teachings have become extremely rare. If I could just acquire copies of its texts, I could ensure its survival. However, in spite of great effort, I've been unable to find any.'

"Wishing to help, Kagyu Tashi searched all over for the texts. From Sharpu Kuga Rinpoche he obtained copies of writings by Kyodrak Chöje on both the path of means and that of liberation. When I had visited the Kyodrak Retreat, Kagyu Tashi had asked me if it would be possible to reestablish the lineage; at the time I had just replied by indicating that he had something of a habitual connection with the Barom. After that, he asked Sharpu Kuga Rinpoche the same question, asking for a divination; he wrote in reply that Kagyu Tashi's two gurus should be encouraged to renew the lineage. One of us, Jamgön Rinpoche, had passed into other realms; there was nothing to be done about that. However, through the effort of the previous Kyodrak Dungkar Rinpoche, copies of Chenngawa's *Four Dharmas* and Tiray's *Collected Writings* existed, and Kagyu Tashi had acquired them.

"He offered me representations of body, speech, and mind, along with five-colored silk, a fine fire-starter, and other things. While presenting these, he asked me to renew the lineage. I prayed one-pointedly to my gurus and chosen deities. In a combination of sleep and the clear light, I encountered the great siddha Matiratna.[81] He was golden in color and wearing the three dharma robes. I explained the situation and prayed to him, and he bestowed through symbol and indication the four profound empowerments, interdependently combining all streams of blessing into one. In my pure perception, I received his secret vajra speech combining all the profound points of the Six Dharmas of Naropa, the path of means.

"Drupgyü Abu Rinpoche opened the door of interdependence allowing me to commit to writing *The Lower Activity of the Wrathful Dark Red Hayagrivakila* and the scroll of *Dorje Trolö, the Subduer of the Haughty* given to me by Nabun the Upasaka. I gave the empowerments for the first time to my son Padma Tsewang, the realized Trime Loden, and other worthy ones.

The deities appeared, and I saw the deities of the complete three seats arise from space and perform the empowerment. When we came to *The Empowerment of the Haughty Ones' Life-Essence,* the outer, inner, and secret eight classes could not bear it.[82] Dark clouds gathered suddenly in what had been a clear sky. Amidst thunder and hail, they actually appeared and earnestly reiterated their previous promises.

"Encouraged by the realized Trime Loden, I committed to writing *The Subtle Drop of Vajrasattva Cycle* that I had brought out of Mayo Snow Enclosure. I also gave the empowerments.

"I went to the lamas' residence at Kyodrak and prepared a Great Thread-Cross of the Dakinis.[83] During this, several wisdom and mundane matrikas appeared, explained what had made them angry, and assured me of their reconciliation with the ceremony's beneficiaries.

"At Sun Moon Cave I performed a Dorje Trolö reversal ceremony. During it, many elementals offered their life-essences.

"When I performed a torma ritual of *The Black Hayagrivakila* in the service of the area of Shotang, I bound by samaya the powerful local spirits.

"I returned to the lamas' residence of Kyodrak. Kagyu Tashi and the others who had previously encouraged me to renew the Barom lineage were joined in doing so by Karma Dulwa, a yogin of the two stages and my disciple; Karma Namdrol; Karma Chökyong; and other thoughtful monks of that monastery. They all urged me in unison, as if with one voice.

"In order that my response to their encouragement not be the misappropriation of dharma or its falsification, I scrutinized my being.

"Lord Langrepa Drakpa Gyaltsen had two principal disciples, one like the sun and one like the moon. The sunlike one was the mahasiddha Matiratna; the moonlike one was the Dharma Lord of Kyodrak, Sönam Zangpo.[84] This is clear in the historical records of this lineage, and is in accordance with my visions. The lineage of the mahasiddha Matiratna has been continued down to the present day as the Oral Lineage of Surmang. I had received it, ripening empowerments and liberating instructions complete in one ceremony, from Tendzin Gelek Nyima, whose kindness is peerless. He bestowed it, including the three profound empowerments, at midnight. I also received it from the Great Abbot Sönam Yeshe, Sangurwa Gonpo Dorje, and Sorak Senge Bum, who were both my masters and my disciples. All of these lines being combined in me, I possessed the authentic long lineage.

"Especially, when I was at Akanishtha Karma Monastery, the supreme place of speech, I had been accepted by the wisdom body of Namkhai Naljorma, the Yogini of Space. One of the four consorts of Lord Lodrö Rinchen, all named Gyen, 'Ornament,' was Yeshe Gyen, the Lady of Tratsa. The Dakini Atroma, who was an actual disciple of Yeshe Gyen, was the consort of the Dharma Lord of Kyodrak, Sönam Zangpo. Namkhai Naljorma was of the same mental continuum as Atroma. From Tsekar Chökyi Drakpa, the lord among siddhas, and from Abo Chökyi Gyaltsen, the Red Repa of Barom, and other siddhas, she received the nectar of their hearts transferred to her as the contents of one vase are poured completely into another. She was the leader of all dakinis of the three places. Through the realization with which she was born and what she had gained in that life through training, she was able to actually go to the land of Uddiyana in the west and receive instructions as quintessential as one's heart from Vajrayogini.

"Namkhai Naljorma, in her wisdom body, bestowed upon me the blessing of her three secrets and the instructions of the profound oral lineage. I therefore possessed an extraordinary visionary lineage of these teachings as well. When Dabzang Rinpoche, our great abbot who was like a second Shakyamuni, was told about this, he placed on my head the flower of his command to propagate the instructions I had received.

"Furthermore, although it is hard to remember every one of my births, I have often remembered being born as Sönam Zangpo, the Dharma Lord of Kyodrak, who was the disciple of Lord Langrepa. While at Kyodrak, I recollected being with my teachers there—how I lived while I was practicing there, what meditation posture and physical exercises I practiced, and how I was so overcome and intoxicated by meditation experience that I acted and spoke crazily, to the point of wearing tattered rags as clothing. I somewhat vaguely remember, like the recollection of a dream, most of my present friends and disciples as connected to me similarly in my life as Sönam Zangpo. It would not be wrong to call that a lineage of recollection.

"Considering all of this, I gained certainty in the appropriateness of my task. Therefore I began the writing on a virtuous and auspicious day at Kyijam Tupten Dongak Shaydrup

Puntsok Dargyay Ling, the Monastery of Kyodrak, at the foot of Kyijam Lion Fortress, a sacred place of body among Tibet's twenty-five sacred places.[85]

"I based it on *The Versified Six Dharmas* by the siddha and protector of beings, Tishri Repa; *The Four Vajra Methods* by Sangwa Lume Dorje; and the instructions on the path of means and that of liberation that are the profound vajra speech of Dharma Lord Sönam Zangpo. I combined the intentions of these into one, and adorned what I wrote with the instruction on the illusory body that I had received in a dream at Karma Monastery while practicing the Karma Kamtsang Six Dharmas, but made sure that the root meditation instructions were identical to those of the Barom forefathers.

"I wrote instructions on the preliminaries, mahamudra, and the Six Dharmas; liturgies for *The Empowerment That Transfers Blessings, The Offering of the Body*, and *The Transference of Consciousness; a Dharma Festival Songbook;* and other texts needed to enable the lineage to stand on its own two feet. All of this was composed at various sites in the Kyodrak area, and was dictated alternately to Kagyu Tashi and Karma Dulwa. Each night during that time, many siddhis appeared to me in meditation and dreams, bestowing instructions. These were the Nyingma siddhas—Vairochana, Kawa Paltsek, Chokro Lui Gyaltsen, So, Zur, and Nup—and the Sarma siddhas—Naropa, Maitripa, Marpa, Mila, Gampopa, Tishri Repa, and Sangwa Rekar. Especially Lord Barompa Tarma Wangchuk appeared. He was so awesome, majestic, and wondrous to look upon that one would never tire of doing so. I therefore think that this work bears tremendous blessing.

"After that I went to gather dairy products and, while doing that, performed service for the nomads of the region. Tsogö Penpo and Dramkar Nyolo displayed their own forms, seeming pleased. Toward the end of that fall, in accordance with Guru Rinpoche's prediction, I performed ceremonies in the service of all Tibet, and also traveled in order to propagate the Golden Dharmas of the Oral Lineage of the Barom Kagyu. While I was in the village of Wa performing service to the whole area, the great local deities, Lord Bomshe and Lord Pakar, appeared as white men wearing armor riding white horses and leading an assembly of all the local deities. They explained their wish to serve and provide for me, and seemed extremely fond of me.

"When I crossed Gyadal Pass and first saw the area of Utse, I saw near the temple there a large white building surrounded by many smaller residential houses. This was the monastery that had been there when, in a previous life, I lived there; I saw it because of my habit from that time.

"On an auspicious day, I was received at the Utse Temple, Pleasure Garden of the Dakinis, by the lamas and custodians. I saw it filled with the dakinis of the three places and an ocean of vidyadharas and siddhas, as numerous as seeds from a burst sesame pod.

"That winter and spring I spent in a cabin at Lion Sky Fortress engaged in the approach and accomplishment of my treasure, *Manjushri, the All-Surpassing Mudra.* All the haughty gods and spirits of the eight classes came to me; I commanded their obedience. They promised, as commanded by the second Buddha,

Padmakara, to serve the Victor's teachings and to actively accomplish the welfare of all the animate and inanimate. At that time, some among my retinue saw, in meditation and dreams, gods and spirits receive samaya.

"During this period, between sessions, I presented to its fortunate first recipients—Kagyu Tashi, Yunying Özer, Könchok Tendzin, the Venerable Tendzin Palzang, and my close companion Jomo Kyi—the ripening empowerments and liberating instructions of the Barom Golden Dharmas that I had committed to writing. I taught Kagyu Tashi all the physical exercises and asked him to eventually teach them to others. During all this, a number of my brother and sister disciples insisted that I sing a vajra song describing my experiences. In the recollection of the lives and kindness of the Kagyu predecessors, and because the door of interdependence was wide open, allowing me to serve the essence teachings, I sang the following song. Composed in a state of exaltation, it is about receiving the close lineage of blessing:

> "NAMO GURU VAJRADHARAYE.
> From this time on until supreme awakening,
> Infallible refuges, three jewels,
> Present in one, omniscient Vajradhara,
> Glorious, mighty Padma—I bow to your feet.
>
> "The kind ones who are not other than him,
> Lords known as the sun and moon,
> The holy father Kagyus, accepted me.
> This is not mere worldly convention.
> They introduced me to mahamudra.

They did this repeatedly, not just once.
They gave me direct instruction like a pointing finger,
Revealing it suddenly, so that I saw whatever
    arose in its nakedness.

"They are the protector Tilopa, a human buddha,
Who united the rivers of the four dispensations;
The glorious, blessed Naropa and Maitripa;
The supreme Hevajra, the translator heruka;
Lord Mila, the source of the lineage of
    accomplishment;
The protector, the single ornament of Jambudvipa,
    called 'the physician,'
The origin of liberation, who united the Middle Way
    and Mahamudra;
His disciple and heart-son, the peerless, glorious
    Barompa—
Is he not Lord Tarma Wangchuk?—
The lineage holders and dharma sons of that supreme one,
The Lords Tishri and Sangwa Rekar;
The holder of the ultimate lineage, Lume Dorje;
And all those in the beautiful, golden garland
That holds the essence of amrita, the river of the
    profound, secret dispensation.

"In the sky of glorious Kirtidhvaja
Shine the sun and moon, the protectors Mati and Punya.[86]
Their disciples and disciples' disciples are shining planets
    and stars.
The brilliant light of the sun never sets.
It warms the lotus of previous karma.

Bees are nourished by its nectar.
The moon, dispelling darkness, circles the four
continents.

"Now is the time when interdependence's design
And the changeless imprint of this line shall appear.
The supreme Vajra Queen appeared as a human
woman in this world
As Namkhai Naljorma, the dakini of the expanse.
In the monastery of terrestrial Akanishtha
She appeared in the costume of a samaya dakini
In order to accept me.
She bestowed, complete in one, the instructions
of the oral lineage,
The profound import of the tantras, and symbolic
empowerment.
I wondered if I wasn't following the tracks of the
father Kagyus.
I gained immeasurable faith and joy.

"In this supreme realm, present from the beginning,
The glorious Heruka and hosts of dakinis have
gathered like clouds.
The herds of siddhas and vidyadharas have blessed us.
Those with and without form have gathered here.
It is like the rock from which a great lion leaps into space.
He surpasses all mundane predators.
The siddha abiding here is victorious.
He has tamed the haughty with his fangs and
claws of a lion.
His power of a lion has grown from within.

He displays his turquoise mane and white coat to
the ten directions.
There will be powerful lion cubs.

"The blessing of the father Kagyus is great.
The river of supreme instruction continues to flow.
I sit at the end of the lineage ranks.
Although the power of my discernment is not great,
I have not fallen from the sky through an extreme
view of the ground.
Although my diligence in the means of meditation
is slight,
I have unified the sun and moon in the path of
luminosity.
Although my courage in yogic discipline is not great,
I have engaged in the conduct that is the means of
unification.
Although I lack qualities pleasing to others,
I have found the result, buddhahood, within myself.
Although it's hard to tame a mind like mine,
The fever of desire has vanished with age.
My weakened mind has lost the teeth of anger.
I surrender victory to the competitive.
I avoid confrontation with the jealous.
I don't much crave wealth.
I may not behave well, but I try to avoid
inappropriateness.
That's my true story.
Because I know myself I can say
There is nothing hidden that could be exposed.
Why should I exaggerate my qualities?

"All my disciples from now on,
Know that the line of instructions from glorious
  Naropa and Maitripa
Is superior to others in its profundity.
This profound path, prophesied by the dakinis,
Comes through a short lineage.
At this time, the end of the third five-hundred-years,[87]
The environment is changing as fast as a field in spring.
The kleshas of its inhabitants are like dust in a tornado.
Their behavior in this decadent age moves like the wind.
Thinking of this, I cry.

"Remember the lives of the father Kagyus.
It's time to relinquish the ambitions of this life.
Meditate according to the instructions of the oral lineage.
Hurry up and practice supreme mahamudra.
All disciples who depend on me,
Don't waste your lives through capriciousness.
Apply your minds to practice.
Don't procrastinate; hurry!
I wish for the interdependence to meet repeatedly.

"That's my answer to my sons' request.
In the pleasant valley of Kyijam, on the bank of the Drichu,
In a place like a great lion leaping into space,
In a spacious cave like the lion's mouth,
I, the last son of the father Kagyus,
Pal Jikme Chökyi Senge,
Have spoken from my heart for the benefit of you disciples.
May the teachings of the ultimate essence spread!

"I composed that spontaneously.

"After that, I performed *The Descent of Blessing for Sacred Places* using *Nangsi Zilnön, the Outer Sadhana of the Guru* from my treasure. I saw innumerable emblems of the bodies, speech, and minds of the boundless, victorious three roots dissolve into everything in the area, down to the smallest pebbles.

"When I left that retreat I went to the palace of Utse, where I offered to the three great tulkus of Kyodrak, and about ten other disciples, the Barom Kagyu empowerment of the five deities of Chakrasamvara. I used the wonderful sadhana and mandala ritual composed by the great glorious Galo, and performed the preliminaries and the actual empowerment together. I also presented *The Empowerment Transferring Blessings* and *The Four Profound Symbolic Empowerments* based on my visions, and *The Wheel of Fire,* the fire and skull empowerments for chandali practice from the Drukpa Kagyu tradition. I offered the Golden Dharmas of the Oral Tradition in their completeness, like pouring all the contents of one vase into another. During all this, with the teachers sitting above, all the viras on the right and all the virinis on the left, we enjoyed a feast gathering in the mandala of Shri Chakrasamvara. I perceived myself as Chakrasamvara and the retinue as the viras and virinis of the mandala. The glorious Four-Armed Protector, the matrika Ekajati, the goddess Vaitali, and other guardians of the oral lineage appeared and actually took the tormas. They promised to guard the holders and teachings of this lineage like their own children.

"After that I went to fulfill the hopes of some patrons. While I was performing service to the people of the Norma Clan of Nangchen, I saw Koro Vajra Rock, on the bank of the Drichu, as the peaceful mandala of *Vajra Space* and the wrathful mandala of *The Sutra of the Vast Assembly*.[88] I became certain, through visions, that Guru Rinpoche, father and mother, had lived there and concealed many profound treasures; that the Dharma Lord of Kyodrak and many other siddhas had practiced there; and that many hand and footprints had been left there. I therefore wrote a guide to the place. There were also indications that my forming a connection to the place would be beneficial to all, and to the people there in particular, so I designed a retreat facility to be built there. The area's guardian, the upasaka Dorje Wangdü Tsal, displayed his own form and, seeming pleased, promised to guard the teachings.

"On the way back to Utse, I drank enough liquor to become slightly intoxicated. While I was in that state, all the local deities of Jambudvipa, headed by Lönpo Kamgyi Jatul, assembled before me. We talked about the features of their respective regions and the customs of the peoples there. At the same time, images of events of the three times arose in my mind like thoughts. I was shocked by the extent of my own cognitive experiences.

"I stopped to rest at a place in Mirti where there was water consecrated by siddhas, and saw the site as a magnificent palace. Above it, in a tent of stainless white cotton, I saw Buddhist deities headed by Vajraheruka, and below that many Bön deities. Continuing on my way, in Trangshung I saw many alloy goddesses, with the heads of vultures, tigers, leopards, and so forth, dancing in all sorts of postures.[89] The whole place, including its fortress, appeared purely to me as Akanishtha and not as this ordinary world.

"In Utse I performed the torma reversal from my treasure, *The Wrathful Guru.* I saw a ghost haunting the Dachu area. He appeared as a monk wearing two woolen cloaks and was surrounded by the ghosts of elderly women, young children, and others. They all appeared after sunset, wailing and calling out. I compelled them and they fled to a great distance.

"One day I went for a stroll, and in front of the monument containing the Dharma Lord Sönam Zangpo's relics, found a definite piece of his bone, the size of one finger-joint. When I saw the tree grown from his hair and the stone called 'The Dakinis' Throne,' I became intoxicated with experience as though with liquor, and saw Lord Sönam Zangpo. Around him were his consort, the dakini Chödzom; his heart son, Balre Rinchen Zangpo; and Marmo Sönam Döndrup. I also saw the rest of 'The Six Dharma Lords Who Equaled Their Teacher'; Beru Yeshe; Palzang, the niece of the Short Lama of Drong; and other supremely holy beings. I vaguely remembered, like remembering a dream, that omniscient Dharma Lord's life, which made me feel both sad and happy.

"On that same day I saw the White Rock of Chabti, on the other side of the Dachu, as the powerful and vast ground of gold that supports the world. On top of it was a Stupa of Many Auspicious Doors made entirely of crystal, its apex reaching into the sky.[90] Within the stupa's vase was Shri Vajrasattva suronded by the boundless Peaceful and Wrathful Ones of Magical Display. Within each of the auspicious gates was one of the buddhas of the ten directions, each surrounded by innumerable bodhisattvas. The stupa was filled from its peak down to its foundation with deities of the three roots, as numerous as sesame seeds spilled from a burst pod. Outside the stupa were all the protectors of localities and treasure, such as the White Realm Protector, gathered en masse and presenting offerings to the principal deities. From all realms in the ten directions, the blessings of the victors were converging on the stupa in the form of five-colored light rays. In particular, coming from the realms in the four directions and the center, five-colored light rays emanated from the hearts of the victors of the five families and were dissolving into the stupa. I witnessed the inconceivably great qualities of the place. The practice place of the Dharma Lord situated there is the equivalent of Lachi, through the interdependence of his having been Jetsun Milarepa in a previous life.

"I saw what I saw through the combination of environment and perceiver. I very much wanted to form a connection with that place, but was unable to because of my age. I feel, however, that it is important for you, my disciples and future followers, to practice in the places where the Dharma Lord Sönam Zangpo lived. Further, all who seek liberation should form as much of a connection with the two sites in that place as you can.[91] If you even prostrate to or circumambulate them, you will give your freedom and resources meaning; this is really important.

"One night around that time, in a dream arisen from luminosity, I saw the whole world clearly, without obstruction. After that, I saw the glorious protector of beings, Barompa Tarma Wangchuk, tell his heart-son, Lord Tishri Repa, that by the bank of the slowly flowing, blue Dachu in Upper Dokham was a place like a blooming lotus. In the flower's calyx was a palace containing the wheels of body, speech, and mind of Chakrasamvara—the residence and residents. In a red palace in Merchung I saw the mother, Vajravarahi, surrounded by millions of dakinis. All the rocks and mountains around Tamrong appeared to me as the boundless display of the form and realm of Manjushri Yamantaka.

"When I was on my way home all the area's local deities attempted to convince me to stay, saying that I should remain there always. Their request was caused by the great connection I had created with them in several lives.

"When I reached Jang Kubum Sershong, I recollected my life as Sangwa Rekar, including his creation of Kubum Tubten Metok Chöling in order to fulfill the wishes of his guru, Tishri Repa. These recollections occurred in images that emerged from luminosity. Along with them came the recollection of the creation of the Black Monastery of Beru and other foundations, all the way down to the number of columns in their temples. I saw all this as a result of my impressions from that time.

"On his way to China, the Fifth Gyalwa Karmapa, Deshin Shekpa, had stayed here. Many spirits came here to offer their magical displays to him. One of them was a malicious spirit from China, who remained here afterward. He later took the form of a Chinese merchant unknown to all, and appeared bearing a column of red sandalwood. He caused discord by successively selling the same column to nine lamas and leaders, including those of Nangsoche, Tsangsar, Beru, and Drong. A monk with perverted aspirations, named Rinchen Öpo, worked with him in full awareness of the discord they were bringing about. That unfortunate monk was tall and pale and wore shoes shaped like a pig's snout. His ghost was still haunting the region maliciously when I was there. Therefore on the day after dreaming all this I dispatched a ransom offering.

"I saw much the same wondrous things there that I had seen at Utse. A vira wearing the costume of a heruka encouraged me to open the place's gate, so I led more than a hundred karma-bearing men and women in circumambulating the place. A lot of food and drink was spontaneously assembled, so I blessed it as undefiled wisdom amrita and performed a feast offering. Boundless pure appearances arose, such as the whole place being filled with the deities and dakinis of the three places. As well, at each of the principal sites, such as the peak, I saw an individual siddha forefather, such as Tishri Repa, the protector of beings. With each of them I discussed dharma and received instruction. I gained the certainty that anyone forming a connection with the place would not be reborn in lower states for at least seven lives. I made the aspiration that in the future one of my followers with the karma and aspiration to do so establish a seat there and spread the teachings; I definitely created the interdependence for this to occur. One day of meditation there will bring more progress than a month elsewhere, so please practice the essence there.

"I saw that the wisdom protectors were still gathered like clouds where the Black Monastery had been. For the sake of interdependence, I initiated a search for the protectors' spirit-stone; a wondrous triangular black stone was found. As requested by the monastic officers and local leaders, I wrote a guide to the place.

"I then went to my monastery, but soon left again in order to perform services for the benefit of an elderly woman of the Achö family of Surmang who had passed away. It appeared to me that she had been reborn in a pure nirmanakaya realm.

"I returned to my monastery and performed for the first time in the newly built residence an Amrita Accomplishment, using *The Sadhana of the Guru's Mind* and *The Guru and the Eight Dispensations* from my treasures. Guru Rinpoche appeared as Uddiyana Vajradhara surrounded by an ocean of vidyadharas and siddhas, and bestowed blessings. I experienced the pure appearance of the whole region as the realm of Lotus Light. When we invited the medicine guardians, I saw the twenty-eight constellations and the eighty goddesses of herbal medicine approach. When we placed the bundles of medicine on the shrine, the dance of alloy goddesses accepting the corpse of siddhi appeared in my mind, so I performed it. All the interdependence at both the inception and conclusion was excellent.

"After that, the door of interdependence was opened by my disciple Trime Loden, and I committed to writing *The Kila of Space.* While doing so, and without the use of rays and so on, the bindu empty lamps appeared clearly and brightly. Inside them was awareness, the vajra chain, shaped like kilas. This appeared continually throughout day and night. I realized the meaning of the penetration of all that appears and exists, all samsara and nirvana, by the kila of awareness.[92] I wrote down on paper *The Kilatantra* and *The Four Activities Relying on the Supreme Sons of the Four Families.*

"Encouraged by the disciple like my own heart, Kyungpo Tulku Karma Gyamtso, I committed to writing *The Life Sadhana Including All Families* and offered the empowerment and transmission to a group headed by that tulku.

"Previously while staying in the home of Anye Orgyen Tendzin in Doyul, a vision came to me indicating the presence of an extraordinary emanation of the omniscient Jikme Lingpa in the direction of the sunset, and that he shared karma and aspirations with me. On the next day I playfully related my vision to my disciple Karma Dondam. I asked him to call to the emanation to come quickly. He went up to the house's roof and called three times with a loud voice. Through that interdependence, the emanation met me while he was very young. I served him through introduction to the nature and so forth. Although he is still limited by his youth, he will definitely be of great service to the Buddha's teachings in general and to my treasures in particular. With the love of a son for his father, he took me as his authority on all the secret points of instruction. I therefore offered him the sincerest advice.[93]

"As prophesied by Guru Rinpoche, through encountering Drolkar, a daughter of the Chungtsang family and rebirth of Shelkar Dorje Tso, I was able to commit to writing the remainder of *The Rishi Loktripala Cycle.* I thereafter performed the empowerments and transmissions for my sons and for disciples like my heart.

"That summer, while traveling to gather dairy products, someone came to invite me to Nemdo Dechen Monastery. I went there and, as instructed by Guru Rinpoche in his prophecies, offered the empowerments and transmissions of *The Rishi Loktripala Cycle.* I performed various services for the benefit of the teachings and that monastery. One night I dreamed that a black man as tall as a tree pointed to a rock to the southeast of the monastery and said, 'A planet-mara lives there; he is responsible.' Since that is the reason for the incidence of planetary illnesses among the lamas and monks of that monastery, I think it is important for them to practice *The Rishi Cycle.* Another night I dreamed that a man wearing a white hat and cloak came down from uphill of the monastery. I asked him who he was, and he said he was the custodian of the fortress of a hundred thousand dakinis. It seems that the mountain behind the monastery is an inner residence of Padmadakini. I wrote a cleansing smoke offering liturgy describing in detail the color and scepters of those dakinis.

"I returned to my own monastery. In the spring of the subsequent year I went to Korok Vajra Rock and exerted myself in establishing the interdependence of the well-being of all Tibet. I made earnest aspirations to that end. As there appeared indications that the continuous practice there of Vajrakila based on my treasures would be beneficial, and as the patrons provided a residence, I formed a connection with the place. For the sake of interdependence I set up an image of the Eleven-Faced Avalokita and established that practice as well.

"I went to Kyodrak Utse. Although there was a prophecy clearly indicating the need to convene a Kila Great Accomplishment Assembly there that year, it did not come about. In its place I performed for seven days a Vajrakila torma reversal in the service of the teachings and beings throughout Tibet. When I performed the suppression of disaster-spirits, there were some signs of benefit.

"I then returned home. Encouraged by the realized Trime Loden, I broke the seal on *The Great Tantra of Yamantaka* and wrote it down on paper. Every time I wrote out the contents of a yellow scroll, different signs of Guru Rinpoche's compassion arose. On this occasion, I vaguely recollected Nupchen's receiving instruction on all the profound points concerning Yamantaka from Vasudhara of Nepal, the discovery of treasure by Gyashangtrom in Yungi Dzalhumo, and other events in previous lives.

"A messenger was sent by the rebirth of the Lord Refuge Lho Rinpoche, inviting me to his residence. I went there and convened a Great Accomplishment Assembly of *Tukdrup Barchay Kunsel.* I offered him most of the empowerments and transmissions from the treasures of Chokgyur Lingpa and many from my own treasures. He was very young, but his personality was that of his predecessor, and he was very affectionate to me. I replaced the old representation of the dharmapala Red Tsiu, which had been damaged. While doing so, that great guardian of the teachings appeared from the north, along with lightning, hail, and thunder loud enough to make your brain explode, and visibly dissolved into the representation.

"I then returned to my monastery and convened a Great Accomplishment Assembly of Vajrakila. During it the usual signs arose, and in particular I received the prophecy that the presence of the Sage's teachings in this place would be of benefit to the teachings and beings throughout all Tibet. Around that time my son, Padma Tsewang, spoke of his experience and realization in the following song:

" 'Namo guru.
Single lord, whose deeds are beyond measure,
First you generated this illusory body of mine.
Then you supported me with material resources.
Ultimately, you showed me the ordinary essence.
To my only father of such kindness,
I offer this spontaneous song of experience
Of the path of generation and completion.

" 'This body is the great mandala of the wisdom
of great bliss.
In the cities of the channels, chakras, and the avadhuti,
I have seen the bodies of deities and the garlands
of syllables.
The vajra repetition, speech like an echo,
Is mantric sound without abiding, coming, or going.
I understand its unceasing vibration of pure speech
To be the expanse of the ultimate vajra sound.
My mind's thoughts, the upsurge of dharmakaya,
Are beyond removal, addition, and craving.
Whatever appears is the great play of wisdom.
I understand whatever arises to be great bliss
beyond action.

" 'When I view this mind that views objects,
The viewer is lost in space.
Awareness-emptiness without center or limit arises.

I have realized that meditation and subsequent
attainment are beyond separation.
When I practice meditation,
Fixation on the act of meditation dissolves in space.
The nature is unceasing.
I understand spontaneously present great openness.
When I practice the conduct,
Fixation on the act of conduct is lost in space.
There is no relinquishment or remedy needed
no matter what arises.
I understand this to be the wisdom of Samantabhadra.
I look forward to wandering in the illusory city of the bardo.
My mind, no self, is without the root of bewilderment.
My body will appear clearly as the real deity.
I want to test my skill in emanation and transformation.

" 'I know that all these external appearances are the play
of mind.
I have realized that this internal awareness is unchanging.
I understand that there is no border between meditation
and subsequent attainment.
My mind's six groups arise without relinquishment
or acceptance.
There is nothing in all of samsara and nirvana to be
accepted or rejected.
In the state free of engagement in imputation
There is nothing to do. I remain without altering
the nature.
I understand that whatever arises is beyond being
stopped or created.

" 'I have cast aside the deceptive dharmas of the
indicative meaning.
I have taken the definitive meaning as my outlook.
Having torn apart the net of dualistic appearances,
I understand that appearances and mind are not two.
Intoxicated by the liquor of the path of bliss-emptiness,
I have untied the knots of hope and fear.
Having built the fortress of no distraction,
I have destroyed the shack of thought.
Having sustained the practice of no fixation,
The craving of fixation has vanished.
Having the meaning of nothing to do in mind,
The bonds of imputation have been cut in resolution.

" 'Through the kindness of my glorious guru and deities,
Delight has been born in my heart.
In the varied appearances of meditation and dreams
I have received introduction through symbols
and words.
While offering a feast at Pomne,
From within the rocks up there
Appeared a dancing blue yogin,
Adorned by jewels and leaves,
Holding a skullcup of amrita'
He said to me, 'Hey! Great yogin! Drink this!'
He gave it to me and I drank it, I dreamed.
In a pleasant meadow at Tsukpu
While in virtuous retreat I saw
The glorious sixth buddha, Mahavajradhara,[94]
Sky-blue and blazing with marks and signs,
Wearing the sambhogakaya costume,

As vivid as a rainbow in the sky.
An inexpressible experience arose.
Bliss and emptiness became inseparable in my mind.
Henceforward, I knew how to sustain wind-mind.
Sometimes agitation and sometimes vague,
Mist-like experiences have continued to arise, but really
Whatever thoughts of pleasure and pain occur,
I have no one else to tell them to but you, father.
Have I achieved practice that can withstand death, or not?
Please continue to keep me in your heart!'

"The arising within my son of such qualities, the result both of his previous lives and of his training in this life, fulfilled my hopes for him. Without distinguishing between day and night, uninterrupted by distraction, his experience had become continuous. A few dreams continued to occur, although only when on the point of awakening from physical sleep. He asked me what to do about them. I offered him the following in answer:

"Hey! Listen, my disciple,
My son, produced by the six elements of my body,
Whom I love more than my eyes and heart,
From early childhood until now
I have supported you in the mundane way with
food and clothing.
I have filled your ears with the dharma of the New
and Old traditions.
I have advised you on what to do with your mind,
and what not to do.
Let that be your inheritance.
Don't waste it; practice it.

"Now you have asked me about your signs of warmth.
I think that your recognition of all dharmas as mind
Is the final resolution of the view.
About the appearance of your external body as a deity,
The spectacles you have seen as the nature of the
internal channels and winds,
The mastery you have gained of non-dual wind-mind,
And your eradication of the dichotomy between
meditating and not—
I think you have mastered the clear light.
In relaxed, natural nothing-to-do,
There is no conduct and no conductor.
There is no hope for peace, nirvana,
And no need to fear existence, rebirth in samsara.
Really, once you are liberated from the net of hope
and fear,
You have achieved the actual result.
When you master emanation and transformation in
the waking state
You can perform these at will while asleep and
dreaming.
You see pure and impure appearances as
entertainment.
Your mastery of the illusory body is clear.
Once you can enter and withdraw from the clear
light in dreams
And whatever you do does not deviate from
awareness-emptiness,
You have accomplished your own benefit.

"Son, this talk of yours is good, not bad,

For you have now accomplished your permanent
well-being.
The hopes of your old father are fulfilled.

"I said that. He later told me that after that, all his sleep became the clear light of dharmakaya. When you consider his experiences, it is as though an old bull became the father of a garuda. Thinking of it, I was genuinely delighted.

"I then gave instruction in the holy dharma of the Great Perfection to many disciples, such as Paldzin Lhamo, a woman of the family of Orgyen Chokgyur Lingpa, and Anye Kyenrap. Especially, I entrusted their direction to the great disciple like my heart, my holy son in dharma, the realized Trime Loden. Each of them gave rise to inconceivable experiences. Nowadays, it seems that innumerable bodies and wisdoms of buddhas appear to everyone around me! These disciples remained in individual retreat cabins, some in dark retreat. They all prayed to me one-pointedly each morning and evening. Through the interdependence of mixing their minds with mine, I was able to know whether or not they had encountered awareness in the manner of rock meeting bone or not. Their thoughts came to me vividly. In the morning and evening, even if I covered my head with clothing, my vision was filled with the appearance of deities and syllables.

"At that time Trime Loden, the yogin of the two stages, spoke of his realization in song:

" 'Indivisible embodiment of all victors, Mahavajradhara,
Düdül Lingpa, conqueror of adversity and darkness,[95]

You who abide vividly in the lotus of my heart—
I offer you the calyx of my undivided faith.

" 'This pure support with eighteen freedoms and resources,
This precious human body has not been wasted.
In reliance on a holy spiritual friend, that excellent
    condition, I received the best method,
The essence of holy dharma, the profound and
    secret sutras and tantras.
I examined these appearances of bewilderment—
Whatever emerged from the unbewildered ground,
The old man of wisdom within my mind—
In both aspect and ultimate nature.
I lay down without care in my own bed, the ground.
I came to know the nature of all the good and bad
    I'd done.
Without complacence due to learning, I applied the
    instructions;
I remained in my seat and analyzed without hope or fear.
In meditation beyond doing, even placement and
    subsequent attainment mixed.
My lack of hesitation in spontaneously writing this song
    of experience
Is due to your kindness, noble one.

" 'The view is the unity of appearance-emptiness
    beyond doer and deed.
Meditation is nonconceptual luminosity, an
    unwavering expanse.
Within it, conduct is yogic discipline beyond
    acceptance and rejection.

Having cast aside this ruinous fixation on a self,
I am automatically victorious over birth and death.
Appearances have become unobstructing, the magical
illusion of relative truth.
Allowing whatever appears as an external object to
liberate itself,
Bewildered thoughts don't truly exist and are empty
of themselves.
Mountains and rocks don't stand up; they are
transparent and penetrable.

" 'The experience of the profound secret of the dakinis,
the connate bliss of melting,
I have cultivated to perfection. Through its illusory
interdependence
I do not crave the pleasure of bewildered appearances;
I revel in great bliss.
The pure nature of the elements and winds is a body
of light.
It is the wisdom display of dharmadhatu, great bliss.
I have experienced the full, undefiled four joys.

" 'Although the word dharmakaya is so renowned,
It refers to nothing more than this very stainless
mind.
Samsara and nirvana are self-liberated and inseparable!
A LA LA!

" 'In that way, my lord, your disciple Padmamati
Presents his experience as a spontaneous song of offering.
Jampal Dorje Tritsun, undisputed great treasure revealer,[96]

Dechen Barway Dorje, I offer this to you.
I request further instruction in the view.'

"This disciple was Lharje Rokchen at the time of Nupchen SangyeYeshe and Repa Shiwa Ö at the time of Jetsun Milarepa. He was closely connected to me as an uncommon disciple in many lives. In this life, after being cared for over a long period by the Lord of Siddhas, Tsoknyi Rinpoche, his karmic disposition arose clearly in dreams and he met me. I offered him all my instructions, such as my treasures, like the contents of one vase being poured into another.

"In response to his song, I composed the following:

"A HO! Trime Loden, holy son of my heart,
The nature of all dharmas is the absence of origination.
You have experienced seeing this directly,
And have relinquished active effort in the transcendence of activity.
You've exposed the lie of the superimposition of samsara, nirvana, birth, and death.
This is the ultimate profound wisdom of Samantabhadra and Vajradhara.
Unceasing naturalness is the primordially pure nature.
Unaltered spontaneous perfection is beyond change and the changed.
Therefore, in the expanse of the dharmakaya, all appearances are pure.
In the all-pervasive, undifferentiated exhaustion of intellect and dharmas,
Great yogi, rest easy and aimlessly.

"Previously, someone had found a black stone by the lake on the near side of Dul Pass. He tried to show it to Tsultrim Puntsok, the attendant of Chusöl Tokden, and to others, but through the activity of the treasure guardian, the Great Naga-Tsen, it reached me via my patron Adro.[97] It was a spirit-stone of Black Jambhala, a precious asmagharbha adorned by dakini symbol-script written by Guru Rinpoche. On its upper portion was a sadhana of Vajrapani; on its middle one of Black Jambhala; and on its lower portion one of the eight great nagas. However, through forgetfulness I had never committed them to writing. Around that time my son Padma Tsewang opened wide the gate of interdependence and my son Könchok Tendzin served as a scribe. However on the day we began to write out the sadhanas, I was on my way north for the last time. I became seriously afflicted by dropsy. My medical attendant was a young woman of the Sharpo Kyangtsang family who eventually gave birth to a boy who bore unmistaken signs of being my son. This boy was accompanied by the dharmapala Red Tsiu like a body by its shadow, and I received the prophecy that he was the rebirth of a good lama of the Drikung Kagyu, and an emanation of Namkhai Nyingpo.

"After that, the rebirth of the Lord Refuge Lhopa Rinpoche came here to my monastery. During our conversations, I mentioned the boy. Lhopa Rinpoche asked me for him, but I did nothing about it.

"Lhopa Rinpoche joined me in the performance of *The Prosperity Accomplishment of Black Jambhala,* during which excellent signs arose. I gave my sons and the others the empowerment for the first time.

"That winter my disciple Kagyu Tashi came from Kyodrak and created an arrow-length likeness of me. In the evening of the day on which it was finished, a number of karmadakinis appeared in my bedroom and told me that the image resembled Jetsun Milarepa more than it did me. They said that this was a result of my karma and aspirations, and that through the blessing of this I would meet Jetsun Shepa Dorje. They then disappeared. In that instant, my entire perception changed and for the length of time it takes to drink a cup of tea, I saw the image, which was in my room, as Jetsun Milarepa. With that pure perception, my devotion blazed immeasurably. After that, I prayed one-pointedly that all who saw the image, even animals, not fall into lower births for seven lives and that they quickly attain omniscience. Since I have vowed this, I think these results of seeing the image are infallible.

"The next morning when I awoke, Kagyu Tashi found a pea-sized, round relic on my bed. As it certainly had not been brought there by anyone, I wondered at first if the relic-locket I wore at my throat had opened up. When I examined it, however, I saw that it had not. I knew then that the relic had come from my body through the force of aspiration. I later placed it inside the image.

"That summer while traveling to gather dairy products, I gave the empowerments and transmissions of Dungtso Repa's *Yangti Single Golden Syllable* at the Kyodrak retreat. Previously I had received detailed instruction in this cycle from the Lord Siddha Lama Rikdzin in Doshul, who asked me to bring its lineage to the Dzagyu area. I gave the cycle in fulfillment of his command.

"As Soktsang Lama Tenchö wished to receive them, I offered him the empowerments of *The Dakini Cycle* from my treasures: the vase empowerment, and the three higher empowerments in their elaborate form. Based on his detailed description of his experiences while practicing this cycle, I think that nowadays siddhas of his caliber are rare.

"On the day I went to Kegi Matramdo, the river turned the color of blood. Five of my disciples assembled, led by Chukduk Bamkyang, and I had the pure perception of the place as the blazing meteoric iron peak of Mount Malaya. As had happened at Senge Zadram, I experienced the boundless pure appearances of the Lord of Secrets teaching the five destined disciples the unsurpassable great secret dharma; I therefore opened the place's gate. On that day I became certain that one of the four great places of refuge concealed by Guru Rinpoche with the present state of conflict in mind was north of there, on the other side of Achen Gangchak. As the signs that it was time to reveal the place had occurred, and the route to the site was clear, I wanted to make the journey in spite of my age in the hope of benefiting beings in this age of degeneration. I explained all this to my retinue of monks, but because their hearts were weak there was nothing I could do.

"I received fine offerings in that area and returned home. That fall I went to Lingru to fulfill the wishes of patrons and to gather grain. Kaydrup, the bursar of Kyodrak, had become terribly ill, and as I was summoned to his side, I went. He and all the tulkus and lamas of Kyodrak had put their trust in me, so I traveled as fast as possible, but still arrived there the day after the bursar's passing. As the three tulkus were quite young, they did not know what to do; I served them through assistance in both the spiritual and mundane aspects of the situation as best I could. Because the deceased had been a person of extraordinary merit, we performed the funeral preparations in the bursary of the lamas' residence exactly as described in the Bamkar text. I also performed a reversal ritual of Yamantaka for the benefit of the whole monastery, and set up a lasting representation for that practice. I performed *The Controlling of Enemies, Death, and Disaster* ceremony at the doorstep of the protector temple at sunset, the time of force. I saw signs of many demons and samaya-corrupting spirits being burnt and falling into the suppression pit in the form of animals such as rabbits. I consecrated an Excellent Jewel representation inside the protector temple during several days. All virtuous spirits, such as the three great nyens of Tibet, assembled. The noble Excellent Jewel and his retinue dissolved repeatedly into the representation. On the last evening Magyal Pomra appeared above the valley in front of the monastery, and said, 'I live at Gyamgyal Guru Colorful Mountain, and from there will assist you.'

"That winter and spring I remained in retreat in the Vajrakila Temple. Through the encouragement of my disciple Yunying Özer and his presentation of a remarkable representation of activity, through the habit of practicing that dharma during many lives, and through the blessing and authorization of my gurus and deities, I wrote down *The Sadhana of the Four-Armed Protector* together with its commentary and permission ceremony. I then gave the empowerment and transmission in the retreat.

"I felt that a monk named Donlo should have been made the

monastery's bursar, but due to the opposition of a few people it did not happen. I attended the Great Accomplishment Assemblies of the monastery and gave empowerments and detailed instruction to those entering the retreat. Then in the summer I left Kyodrak, traveling briefly to gather dairy products, and then easily reached my home.

"At that time all of Tibet was involved in a great conflict. A great army from China was approaching Tibet, led by a general known as Yaktruk. He had conquered the eighteen districts in the east and all districts west of them up to Black and White Khyungpo. Many of the greatest monasteries of Tibet had been sacked and destroyed. This large army from China had appeared in Ga, and many of the area's leaders had been deposed. Chingtu Rinpoche was forced to go there. I was extremely concerned, and sent my son Padma Tsewang with a scarf of greeting. When I had previously restored the stupa of Ridong, the protector Kugyal Shene gave me a piece of the stupa. I sent this as an offering to Chingtu Rinpoche for the interdependence of political stability. He sent back a generous gift and his assurance that he was in no physical danger. From that time on, I was unable to travel and remained in retreat praying all day and night for the protection of all Tibet and especially of our region. In particular, I performed the protection and reversal rituals of the Shvanas from my treasures and the forceful thread-cross ritual of White Umbrella. Signs of benefit were manifested.

"Since the protector of the invaders from the borderlands was the god Maheshvara, I befriended him, as Guru Rinpoche had commanded me in his prophecies. I gained control of

Maheshvara's vital force, and earnestly entrusted him with activity. I became aware of spirits sent to destroy the Buddhadharma by many non-Buddhist siddhas. I gave them offerings and turned the curses back onto their originators. This and the magic performed by other lamas affected Yaktruk, who was executed by decapitation. Chingtu Rinpoche returned in good health from central Tibet; in celebration I invited him to my monastery and served him there. As instructed by Guru Rinpoche, for the welfare of all Tibet, I instituted the regular performance at my monastery of Great Accomplishment Assemblies of *Vajrakila, The Sadhanas of the Guru's Mind,* and *The Dakini Sadhana.* As Great Splendor Chakrasamvara is extolled for the purpose of taming borderlands and barbarians, Padma Tsewang and I together performed that practice, with elaborate offerings.

"Nyindzong Trichen and Trizur came to my monastery, and I offered them some empowerments and transmissions from my treasures.

"At that time I placed the appropriate dharanis in my likeness made by Kagyu Tashi, and also consecrated and venerated a wondrous self-arisen image of Guru Rinpoche I had acquired, as well as an embroidered depiction of me, the relic that had appeared on my bed, and other special representations, using *The Sadhanas of the Guru's Mind.* The signs of virtue were good.

"That fall, the rebirth of the Lord Refuge Lhopa Rinpoche came to my monastery. I offered him a life-empowerment and some significant practical instruction.

"As Chingtu Rinpoche remained anxious about the conflict with China, I requested Taklung Matrul Rinpoche to perform a divination. As a result, he sent a messenger to tell me that it would be beneficial for me to perform whatever ceremonial service I felt would help our land, and that I should go to the capital of Nangchen for that purpose. However, on the night his messenger reached me, Ekajati, the Guardian of Mantra, clearly told me that it would be best if both my patrons and I remained in retreat as we had promised. I therefore excused myself from the journey. I performed a seven-day Great Accomplishment Assembly of Yamantaka, sponsored by Chingtu Rinpoche. Extraordinary signs of force arose, such as the water-bowl offerings turning to blood.

"Because of my extreme age and resultant poor vision, and because I had no plans for the future with regard to either dharma or the mundane, and no anxiety about the completion of any past endeavors, by this time all elaborations in thought and activity beyond the three concerns had spontaneously ceased.[98] I abided in the yoga of space beyond action, awaiting death. The great Jetsun Milarepa said, 'There is nothing that cannot arise in a yogin's experience; there is nothing that won't grow in a summer field.' As he said, there is nothing that I had not experienced in my life. By this time, the amount of time it takes to drink a cup of tea could appear to me as a period of months or years, and all good and bad thoughts were like the spell of an illusionist. There is no particular need for anyone to hear about how this developed, and in any case it is impossible to describe, but to merely give you the seed of an idea of it, it was like this:

"First of all, light issuing from my fingers caused the appearance of innumerable realms on the surface of each of my fingers. The light then seemed to spread, engulfing my residence and all the nearby buildings, rocks, and mountains, until I could see everything without obstruction, like a wet kyurura fruit in the palm of one's hand. I heard what anyone said as though it was said right next to me. At times, I was amazed by my own experience; at other times, I grew tired of it. It continued to expand until I could see China, Nepal, and, in particular, a huge country to the north that I think might be Shambhala, surrounded by snow-covered mountains. That country has large forests, many large and small rivers, with an inconceivable variety of settlements in between them. Eventually I could see all the way to the ocean around Jambudvipa, and across it to a land that I think might be Langkapuri, the rakshasa land, where all the mountains and rocks are red, and where the many cities are made up entirely of buildings constructed of red brick. I saw innumerable islands of many different kinds, and the eastern continent of Superior Form. Its mountains are all round at the top, and all its valleys are white in color. Each of its peaks is adorned with a rainbow halo; in between them are lakes, all perfectly round like water-offering bowls. The many beings that live there enjoy inconceivable sense-pleasures. All their garments are white.

"In that way, I saw all the four continents and eight islands. I would become so involved in these appearances that I was insensible to our ordinary appearances. As this occurred repeatedly, my attendants had to shake me and remind me to eat and go to sleep. Until they did so, I would neglect to do these things. I was unaware of my residence and seat. People began to suspect that

I had become senile. In fact I had left behind all thoughts of fixated perception, such as those of my bed, room, and walls; naturally this affected my behavior to some extent.

"Late one night I saw what I think was a god realm. Indra, the ruler of the gods, was riding an elephant surrounded by his thirty-two deputies and many others traveling to the north. I saw many appearances of the six states. When I saw the ripened karma of innumerable suffering beings in the hells, the preta lands, and so forth, uncontrollable compassion arose in me. Observing the behavior of most of us, who merely pretend to be practicing dharma, I was displeased and for more than a year was tormented by such unbearable sadness and disgust that I cried all day and night. I had no interest in talking to anyone and would only recite mantras and the names of buddhas.

"As I saw clearly that our present state of conflict is nothing more than the result of our karma, I practiced giving and taking in a state of love and compassion throughout the day and night. I dedicated mani mantras to Yaktruk and the rest of the Chinese armies. I came to think it would be best if others did this too.

"One day, unobstructed by buildings or other regions, I saw a high mountain. On its peak was the noble White Tara, with her seven eyes of wisdom appearing distinctly. One morning, I saw Lord Dusum Khyenpa surrounded by the ocean of Kagyu siddhas. I saw many gurus and siddhas of the past.

"Then I saw, clearly and distinctly, the realms and bodies of many buddhas and bodhisattvas in the ten directions, including their passing and abiding. As a result, faith and devotion increased in me and blazed without effort. I repeatedly felt like telling others of the qualities and deeds of these buddhas and bodhisattvas.

"All of these appearances were vivid appearance without reality, like reflections in a mirror, and appeared of themselves. They were therefore not a source of bewilderment.

"Then my disciple Yunying Özer came from Kyodrak. We talked of the appearance of visions, and I said the following about my realization:

> "In the vast ocean of buddha nature
> The little fish of mind itself, with the golden eyes of
> awareness,
> Flaps the six wings of the inner faculties.
> The outer faculties move about in the ten directions.
> If the outer and inner retain this golden gleam
> Object and subject are powerful and not two.
> Self-awareness is the perfect buddha! EMAHO!
> May this be realized by myself and all beings!
> This was composed by Dechen Barway Dorje.
> May all attain buddhahood.

"In response, he asked me, 'To what realm are you going to go?'

"I replied, 'I'm not going anywhere, not up, not down, not in any direction. Since I'm not going anywhere, I won't be returning from anywhere. Once these appearances of self-awareness are purified, all that appears is the dharmadhatu.'

"Samantabhadra, without having performed a hair's worth of virtue, awakened of himself, and his wisdom self-appearance is all pervasive. All sentient beings, without having performed a hair's worth of wrongdoing, became deceived by the thought of apprehended and apprehender and wander in the inexhaustible bewilderment of the karmic appearances of attachment, aversion, and apathy. Really, once you realize that samsara and nirvana are like the front and back of your hand, and you experience authentically in your heart the separation of bewilderment and liberation, you see that what we call 'birth' and 'emanation' amount to the same thing.

"For example, I began to appear to myself sometimes as female and sometimes as male. This is because of the imprints within my mind, which includes both the mind of Nupchen Sangye Yeshe and that of Yeshe Tsogyal. The dispatching of emanations is just like that. In some realms I am dying; in some I am being born; in some I am active. Because I have gained the certainty that it is all emanation and like magical illusions, I do not feel that I abide in any limitation.

"Then all those appearances changed, becoming the display of the five wisdoms—rainbow light, drops, little drops, and horizontal and vertical spokes of light—all of this boundless, a vast expanse filling all space above, below, and around me. Within this appeared the primordial buddha, Samantabhadra; the peaceful sugatas such as Shri Vajrasattva; and the wrathful blood-drinkers such as the Supreme Heruka. Their innumerable bodies of light were of all sizes from as large as mountains to as small as mustard seeds. They filled my field of vision, obscuring ordinary appearances. Among them were the forms of buddhas and bodhisattvas, some two- and some three-dimensional. Whole strings of these forms appeared repeatedly, moving and shaking. Sometimes, such as when I was basking in the sun's warmth, there appeared strings of blue vajras, each the size of a standing person, as though they were suspended in the sky. Lattices of light filled the sky; walls, doors, and other surfaces both inside and outside buildings were covered by countless drops of five-colored light, white svastikas, and vermillion joy-swirls, all of them spinning. Innumerable forms of the twenty-eight Ishvaris, large and small, and graceful with the nine awesome moods, filled everywhere I looked, dancing.[99] I would become diverted by their dance movements. At night, all those daytime appearances would continue vividly, without interruption. As this lasted for between four and five years, I cannot describe every detail of the appearances.

"As well, sometimes the inside and outside of my residence became filled with women among whom were a few with the eye of wisdom. They would appear like an optical illusion, passing their time there in a state of pleasure and delight. At those times, my attendants and some of the monks would hear the voices and laughter of women.

"One day, just after my morning tea, three women entered my room. When I looked directly at them, I saw that they had three eyes. As their leader also had a joy swirl of vermilion on her forehead, it was certain that, if I had embraced her, I would have reached the celestial realm on that very day. However, in the hope of being of some further use to the beings and teachings of Tibet, I let the opportunity pass.

"Since the reign of King Langtarma, every Fire Dragon Year has been unlucky for Tibet. In my youth, it was during that year that the terrible conflict with Nyarong occurred.[100] I became fearful for the welfare of the beings and teachings of all of Tibet in the next Fire Dragon Year.[101] I therefore committed to writing *The Great Feast Dance of the Dakinis,* as instructed by my gurus and deities. I taught it to Kagyu Tashi, who taught others. Sponsored by him, Namdröl Zangpo, and other disciples from Kyodrak, a Great Accomplishment Assembly was convened. The feast dance was inserted into its conclusion, and was performed in its most elaborate form by me, my sons Padma Tsewang and Trinlay Palzang, Tsewang Namgyal, and others—almost a hundred of us. During it, these ordinary appearances were torn away. In the great secret bhaga of the Vajra Queen, in the presence of the great lord of the six families, Vajradhara, we all appeared purely to me as male and female herukas enjoying the feast gathering. As well, hosts of viras and dakinis of the places and realms gathered like clouds and blessed the participants, the place, and all the offerings. I also saw the male and female samaya-bound ones take the tormas of command. At the same time, the guardian Tongtrom Kanye came from the shady side of Danyin Mountain. The perception of everyone attending, young and old alike, was utterly transformed. They gained undivided faith and were amazed. I entrusted the responsibility of the future continuation of the feast dance assembly to Kagyu Tashi, Karma Chökyong, and Karma Namdröl. Seeing signs that the celebration of it at Kyodrak would be beneficial locally and in general, I encouraged them to establish it there.

"From the time when we convened that assembly, the appearance of many women in my residence increased greatly. My rooms became filled day and night with the sound of drums, conch shells, cymbals, lutes, and flutes. My attendant of authentic family Kalzang Drönma, and most of those for whom these ordinary appearances are a thin veil, heard it.

"As this old man was able to defer that year's ill fortune, I was quite useful to all for someone who was almost a corpse. However, as a result my household experienced great upheaval caused by the curses of barbarians. My son Padma Tsewang passed away at the age predicted by Taklung Matrul Rinpoche in his recognition letter. As I was in retreat for a month and a half at the time, I entrusted the responsibility of the necessary arrangements to my sons Trinlay and Kunzang. They invited Surmang Tendzin Rinpoche, who conducted the cremation. My attendant Jomo Kyi saw within the cremation smoke Padma Tsewang, bright white in color, naked, dancing gracefully in space. It is therefore certain that he had gone to the celestial realm. Around that time Söpal, who had great faith in my son, saw him as he had appeared in life, wearing his robes and hat, but brightly luminous and majestic. Each of those with faith saw a different pure appearance. Many deities and syllables appeared on his bones and relic pills as well. In particular, the appearance of sindhura among his relics indicates his attainment of the celestial realm. Lhopa Rinpoche and lamas from Kyodrak and Surmang were invited and we offered them as much as we could.

"Some people criticized me for not officiating at the funeral services on account of the feast dance assembly, but it was not my intention to be callous or disrespectful. For one thing, the performance of the feast dance was the instruction of my gurus and deities; for another, I was definitely sent to Tibet by Guru Rinpoche for its benefit. If, in the fulfillment of the slightest command of the second Buddha, my body were ground to dust, I would have no regret. So please know that it is extremely important that the feast dance be celebrated yearly from now on.

"That summer my disciples Yunying Özer and the young woman called Shri came from Kyodrak. They said they viewed me, their root guru, as a buddha, and asked me to 'openly reveal my qualities.' The victors and their children cause their blessings to enter into those called 'lamas' for the benefit of their disciples. In that way it is the victors and their children who care for disciples through their guru. It is therefore unfitting to doubt one's teacher. It is hard for anyone other than those with karma and good fortune to see their guru's qualities as they are, because we project our own faults onto others. It is like someone with jaundice seeing a conch shell as yellow.

"I replied to their request, 'If I were to explain my qualities, it would be a description of the three gates to liberation.[102] When your realization of the nature of things matures, you will see them for yourself. Until then, it will be hard for you to understand them.'

"Previously, when I had first gone to Kyodrak, I had wondered if there might not be a powerful 'eye of the land' there. On my way to the existing retreat facility, I looked for it. I found what is called in the Chinese system of geomancy a 'dragon's eye of the land.' I felt that it would therefore be excellent for an additional retreat facility to be built there. However, this did not happen back then. Now the interdependence for a retreat hall to be built there was present. Since the features of the site ensured the great benefit of beings and the teachings, I provided the necessary funds and resources and ordered its construction.

"One night, in a dream arisen from the clear light, my body had wings like a bird. I flew ever higher into the sky, followed by many like me, flying in single and double formation. We filled the sky like birds driven into flight by a stone from a sling. On the ground below were countless beings calling me by name, crying, bowing, lying prostrate with misery, and wailing. Seeing them, unbearable compassion arose in me, and I made the earnest aspiration to take care of them all myself.

"If you who follow me remain inseparable from the yoga of the two stages that I have taught you, you children will follow in your father's footsteps. That dream appears to have been a sign that I will greatly benefit many beings of all types in the future.

"One time I appeared in sambhoghakaya costume, seated on the great lion throne of fearlessness. Devas, nagas, ghandarvas, kumbandhas, humans, and all other beings of the six states were assembled at once. I taught dharma both vast and profound to all of them simultaneously, in one language and with one voice. They each heard it according to their individual capacity. This is all the infallible and profound result of my repeated gathering of the accumulations and repeated making of aspirations since I first generated bodhichitta for beings' benefit countless lives ago. Therefore my followers, be earnest in that intention and its application.

"In the fall the Lord Refuge Drongyül Rinpoche's rebirth came to meet me; I gave him the empowerments of *The Life Sadhanas* from my treasures and the entrustment ceremony for all my treasures. I was too old to do more than that myself, but I had my eldest son, Trinlay Palzang, offer him all the other empowerments, such as those of *Yamantaka.* As the previous Drongyül Rinpoche was a predicted inheritor of many of my treasures, this was like the reunion of father and son; our minds were united in both dharma and mundane matters. This was a further fulfillment of Guru Rinpoche's aspirations; this excellent, virtuous interdependence brought joy to this old man's heart. I became hopeful that Drongyül Rinpoche would accomplish the two benefits in the manner of the waxing moon through this dharma. I made that aspiration, invoking the power of the truth.

"After that, Garwang Choktrul Rinpoche came from Surmang. He was greatly interested in my *Yamantaka* treasure, which was most appropriate from either a dharmic or a mundane perspective. As this old man considered him part of my family, I had him stay in my residence. The evidence of my service to Surmang is visible to all with discernment. All the old monks of that monastery with interest in the inner meaning are my disciples. The two supreme incarnations upholding its teachings have been like my own heart in both their former and present lives. From the time of Lord Nupchen up to now, my secret yidam, like my life force, has been *Manjushri the All-Surpassing Mudra.* My root guardian has been the matrika Ekajati, her sadhana combining the treasure and oral traditions in one. Since it was certain that these two practices would benefit the Surmang teachings, I offered the samadhi empowerments and entrustment of instructions in a spirit of gratitude for the opportunity to do so. I entrusted Garwang Rinpoche with the responsibility of upholding, sustaining, and propagating these teachings. I asked him and Surmang Tenga Rinpoche to guard my seat and treasures.

"My son Trinlay Palzang and his son returned from their journey to the north with a copy of the Narthang edition of the precious words of the Buddha, which had been consecrated with grain from the hands of the sixteen noble elders and therefore bore especially great blessing.[103] In appreciation I offered him, his son, and his younger son eight measures of silver, and he left the books here.

"In mid-spring of the next year Kagyu Tashi returned. He corrected the dancing of my monastery's monks. With my son Trinlay Palzang and his son presiding, *The Great Feast Dance of the Dakinis* was performed in the context of a Great Accomplishment Assembly. As in the previous year, the three gatherings occurred.[104] In particular, the melody of songs sung in the symbolic language of the dakinis was heard by all, day and night, like the buzzing of bees. Rainbow light of the five wisdoms' colors, both horizontal and vertical, filled my residence, the temple, and the surrounding area. Rainbow clouds gathered in the sky. Many such wondrous signs appeared to many fortunate people.

"After that Kagyu Tashi performed the approach of *The Life Sadhana Including All Families* for my benefit for three weeks.

Immediately after that my two sons, Trinlay's son Tsewang Namgyal, the realized Kagyu Tashi, and others offered one hundred life-ransoming offerings and a great torma for the Lord of Death, and performed *Turning Back the Call of the Dakinis.* In that ceremonial context they also requested me to remain and accompanied all this with extensive material presentations.

"The Lord Refuge Taklung Matrul Rinpoche said, 'As was predicted to Chingtu Rinpoche, the well-being of all Tibet and especially of our region depends upon you, my lord. Although we have suffered the disturbance, like boiling water, of an invasion from China, thus far the meditation communities have not been harmed, as though they were golden articles hung out of reach in the sky. We cannot measure your kindness in fulfilling the predictions about you. Therefore please consider our unanimous petition that you remain among us so that the sun of our happiness does not set. All of us who are your disciples beg you a hundred and a thousand times to keep your lotus feet firmly placed with a vajra knot.'

"I replied, 'Attachment to these aggregates and elements at my great age has been taught to be the greatest suffering of human beings. It is indeed troublesome. However, if I definitely possess the good fortune to be of benefit to others, may all victors and their children bring it about. Still, Milarepa, the lord of yogins, said, "The work of this old man is done. Your time has come, my great children." Like him, I have no real regrets based on not having done whatever I could for the benefit of myself and others, or on not having achieved something in particular. The essence of my benefit for others is the several profound treasures that I have revealed through the aspiration of Guru Rinpoche, father and mother. This is due to their kindness alone. From now on, my followers, trust in these treasures. Teach them. Study them. Meditate on and practice them. Be appropriately diligent in this. Whether I live or die, I've no more to say or do than this.'

"In particular, Trinlay's son Tsewang Namgyal is an emanation of the monk Namkhai Nyingpo as predicted by Guru Rinpoche. According to my own visions, he appears also to be an emanation of Sönam Özer, the heart son of the Barom Kagyu siddha Sönam Döndrup. According to both worldly and dharmic traditions, he holds my lineage and will surely accomplish the two benefits with distinction. In consideration of this, I presented the complete ripening empowerments and liberating instructions of the Barom Kagyu Golden Dharmas from my visions to him and to all the worthy ones present there. Kagyu Tashi's eyes took the place of my own.

"There have been several predictions that it would be of great service to the meditation communities of upper Dokham if the Source of Amrita Stupa and the Raksha Nang Stupa, both erected by Guru Rinpoche in order to tame the border areas, were restored. The necessary circumstances have not yet arisen, but I still feel it would be worthwhile.

"As I had instructed the previous year, my disciples at Kyodrak celebrated the Dakinis' Feast Dance at Kyodrak Sun Moon Cave. It went well, and wondrous indications of its benefit for beings and the teachings arose.

"After my disciples dispersed, it became evident that some

people from my area who had gone on pilgrimage to Kawa Karpo had brought the black pox back with them. Before anyone had become aware of it, it had spread, and at least nine people, including the infant son of a woman from the Sharbu family, had died. We all became afraid. I practiced giving and taking with concentrated bodhichitta to the best of my ability. It seemed that anyone who had contracted and survived the white pox was immune to the black pox. I had previously contracted and almost died from the white pox when I was in Drakyap in the service of the holy son of the Terchen. Nevertheless I contracted the black pox now, and became very ill. From the time I became ill, twenty-one men and women who were suffering from the disease began to recover, and the epidemic ceased. It seems you could say that I actually took upon myself the suffering of others.

"At that time I turned over the responsibilities for the performance of our monastery's various communal services and assemblies, such as funerals, to my sons, who were very helpful. I became weak from the illness, and that, together with my great age, made me unable to rise from my bed. I could consume no solid food, and only took tea and a little melted butter. While I was in this state, Kalzang Drönma, the rebirth of Nanamza, took care of me with the persistence and courage of a mother caring for her child. Really, from the time we first met, she undertook every possible service of the three gates. During my illness, she spoke to me in a state combining love and sadness. I responded with this advice:

> "Kalpika, my friend like my own heart,[105]
> You have been karmically connected to me since your youth.

I have given you earnest instruction and introduction.
I think there is no instruction remaining to be given.
However, I have three things to say in response to
    your kindness.
Don't forget them; keep them in your heart.

"All composites are like magical illusions and dreams.
Especially these aggregates that we cherish are fragile.
Life is impermanent, like a candle in the wind.
Don't deceive yourself with the assumption
    of longevity.
Right now excellent causes and conditions are present.
Don't waste these three gates.
Practice generation, mantra, and completion to the
    extent of your knowledge.
If, undeceived by the bewilderment of distraction,
You continue until death, that is enough.

"This naked, unborn nature of mind,
Never without mindful awareness—
Sustain this experience like a river's current.
If at night you are unsullied by the bewilderment
    of dreams,
And in the day unobscured by thoughts of the
    three poisons,
That is maturity of experience.
Until these indications arise in your being,
Daughter, exert yourself!
Devotion without fluctuation
And samaya without pretension—
Don't forget these! Keep them in the center of your heart!

"From our first meeting until now
You have never cast me from your mind.
That is the fulfillment of this old man's hopes.
I will never abandon my love for you.
Don't forget that! Aspire that we be inseparable!

"Look at this single mind itself in the present,
Viewing it as indistinguishable from me.
Meeting and parting don't really exist; that is the
nature of things.
Resting freely is your mind's natural condition.
Give rise to certainty unsullied by doubt.
Practitioner of dharma, practice this!

"Although I have no real attachments, in accord with mundane custom I also gave advice to my closest monks and disciples. In that year, on the tenth day of the third month of autumn, he of peerless kindness, the great treasure revealer and king of dharma, Orgyen Chokgyur Lingpa, came to receive me with a retinue of viras and dakinis from the places and lands.[106] Various visions came to me. I said to my disciple Padma Trime Loden, 'There were indications in the past that if I directed my aspirations to the celestial realms, I could have gone there without leaving any aggregates behind. Because, for the benefit of beings and the teachings, I did not do so, I will have to leave this form aggregate behind. Today, this old man has seen clear signs of passing on. Set up a high throne, place me on it, and set out elaborate feast offerings.'

"He began to cry out of great sadness, and said, 'Consider with kindness the desperate beings of this degenerate age! Don't depart to the expanse of peace! We have prayed for you to remain for a long time!'

"He said that and more, and performed the most meticulous ceremonial service. Although I cannot claim to have control over my life and death, as a result my body and awareness did not separate then.

"In the midst of spring a number of monks and disciples came, led by Kagyu Tashi. They told me that on the day that the signs of death appeared to me, the lord of siddhas, Tenchö, told his attendant Karma Namdröl, 'Viras, dakinis, and virtuous devas and nagas are talking about escorting Barway Dorje to the pure celestial realms. If you pray to him now there will be great blessing.' The disciples asked me the reason for this. I told them and they were delighted.

"I entrusted Kagyu Tashi with the correction of texts containing liturgical arrangements of my treasures. To the others I pointed out the Great Perfection and blessed them. I entrusted their future instruction to my son in dharma, Padma Trime Loden. The lineage of my treasures, of Dungtso Repa's *The Single Golden Syllable of Black Yangti,* of 'The Sealed Profound Varahi' from *The Northern Treasures,* and the rest, had been established. Many disciples had gained the signs of warmth on the path.

"At that time Gar Rinpoche, Könchok Tendzin Gyalway Nyugu—the rebirth of Gar Chödingwa, the heart son of the Great Dharma Lord of Drikung—came to me accompanied by Kalzang Chödrön and other disciples. He had been instructed by Drongyül Rinpoche, Orgyen Nüden Dorje, to go to meet me, but had been too busy to do so. After that, he had decoded many symbolic instructions of dakinis, and so earnestly said to me, 'I need the empowerments and transmissions of all your profound treasures.'

"Although I wished to fulfill his request, I have never dared to designate as inheritors of my dharma persons of high standing on that basis. I have done so only on the basis of previous aspiration and prediction. My only responsibility has been to write out whatever I found and practice it to the best of my ability. The extent of beings' benefit has depended on Guru Rinpoche's aspirations and intentions. Someone such as myself could not hope to achieve anything beyond that even through great effort and fine speech. Certain of this within the depths of my heart, I have lived simply, as everyone knows. Furthermore, by this time I was so old that it was not possible for me to offer him the treasures individually.

"Many past treasure revealers, however, such as Ratna Lingpa, had imparted empowerment through samadhi and the sovereignty of their dharma to predicted inheritors simply through meeting them or even through a letter. In that way they sent the chariot of their activity in a hundred directions. So, using the eyes of Kagyu Tashi as substitutes for my own, I offered Gar Rinpoche the empowerment of *The Life Sadhana Including All Families* and, within it, the entrustment of all the instructions of the secret treasures. Since he was a predicted inheritor of *The Dakini Cycle* and *The Manjushri All-Surpassing Mudra Cycle,* the excellent interdependence of the father's wealth being passed to the son was established. I received from him *The Life Empowerment of White Tara* according to the Drikung tradition. During it, he performed a ceremony for my longevity. He also presented generous offerings.

"Kagyu Tashi led the yearly Great Accomplishment Assembly of the Dakinis with *The Great Feast Dance,* as in the past.[107] Because I was on the point of the dissolution of the appearances of this life, I considered myself extremely fortunate to have been able to attend three yearly celebrations of the feast dance. It is the quintessence of the ocean of dakinis and the profound mother tantra taught by Guru Rinpoche, the second Buddha, and convened at this seat of Darong Blazing with Mountains of Fire, the great place of the dakinis. I felt great joy in thinking that the wishes of Guru Rinpoche, father and mother, had been correctly fulfilled. Anyone who sees *The Great Feast Dance,* unsullied by doubt, and practices dharma in accord with dharma, will be reborn in the feast ranks of the dakinis in Uddiyana.[108] Therefore, do so!"

In that way, I was fortunate to hear the garland of amrita, the account of his life, from the lotus petals of the supreme, noble guru's mouth. That completes the second part.

Virtue in the End

The Conclusion of the Autobiography

At around that time, the lord guru began to develop bedsores and blisters in his lower body. We all perceived him as becoming progressively more and more ill.

On the eighteenth day of the third month in the Male Earth Horse Year, the Lord of Siddhas Shasadharma passed away at Kyodrak in order to benefit beings elsewhere.[109] He had been the principal disciple of the Lord Refuge Dungkar Rinpoche, and had recently received from the lord guru, as predicted by deities, the uncommon three profound empowerments in connection with the empowerment of *The White Khechari of Great Bliss.*[110] His mind had mixed with that of the lord guru. As I, Kagyu Tashi, was the least of disciples of those two holy beings, a messenger arrived, with a horse for me to ride, summoning me to Kyodrak. I explained this to the lord guru, and he replied, "I don't know how long I'm going to live either, so stay here for a few more days to ask me any remaining questions you have, for the sake of your mind's satisfaction."

By that time, in the perception of most of his disciples—such as she of authentic family, called Shri—the lord guru's bedroom and especially the area around his form were filled with five-colored rainbow light, drops of light, tiny drops of light, vertical rays of light, and horizontal ones. Some of this was vivid and some not. At the same time there was an indescribable sound that was barely audible, a little like the distant buzzing of bees, that continued day and night.

At times the lord guru appeared ill, at times semi-conscious, and at times he seemed to sleep throughout the day and night. However, aside from his inability to rise from his bed or sit up, his mind displayed none of the infirmity associated with advanced age, and he did not appear to be suffering at all through illness. He remained cheerful and at ease.

I asked him about the signs we were seeing and hearing and about what he was experiencing. He replied, "From the time when I was first accepted by the great revealer of treasure, the king of dharma, Orgyen Chokgyur Lingpa, and all the way up to now, I have taken ati, the Great Perfection, as my path through aspiration. What you are seeing and hearing may be internal signs manifesting externally. However, as for what I am experiencing, all my previous experiences have been exhausted. Thoughts of dharmas have mostly dissolved into dharmata, the non-composite nature, the primordially pure expanse of the Great Perfection, like the disappearance of the waning moon into space. There is no longer any apprehension of anything as 'this' or analysis of anything as 'not this' for me. You could call this the 'exhaustion of intellect and dharmas.'[111] In my experience now there is not so much as an atom of anything to meditate on and not so much as an instant's distraction. All the bewilderment of day and night has been purified of itself. I think there is nothing wrong with calling this 'no meditation.'[112] As the sensations of my physical body arise as the display of emptiness, I am immersed in that, and experience no discomfort whatsoever. The withstanding of conditions and the thoughts of birth and death are for me like the contents of a dream from which one has awoken. So even if I die today I will have no fear or anxiety. After all, the destruction of these composite aggregates happens to everyone; it therefore must happen to me. However, at the conclusion of the Life Sadhana and reversal rituals you're doing, it would be good for you to give me another life empowerment."

I felt that it was most unfitting for me to do so, considering that he was my guru and actually a buddha, but not knowing his reason for the request I also could not refuse. So I did it, after which he also gave me a life empowerment. He then placed the wish-fulfilling jewel *Fulfillment of All Wants and Needs,* which he had discovered as treasure, on top of my head. He then said, "All of you great beings, predicted as inheritors of my treasures, especially my son, Kunzang Dorje, and you—collect these teachings and put them in order. Do this as best you can, and the hopes of this old man will be fulfilled. You will have served the teachings of Guru Rinpoche. The sons will have upheld their father's dharma, my son."

I asked him who would appear as predicted inheritors. He

replied, "Yeshe Tsogyal said, 'All in the future with interest in the treasure dharma will be those who have met Guru Rinpoche now and made aspirations. You are all endowed with karma, so rejoice! These words of mine are more precious than gold.' As she said, although it is possible for followers of these teachings to be perceived by others as either good or bad, anyone with faith and interest in these treasure dharmas, anyone who practices them, is in a sense a predicted inheritor of my dharma. The signs of this will manifest. Led by you great disciples, all those who follow my lineage now and in the future are entrusted with the teachings of these secret treasures of the essence, which are like wish-fulfilling jewels. Practice them yourselves and use them to take care of others." In that way, he gave much final advice.

Then feeling that he would not remain among us much longer, I asked him to bestow his advice to all who depended on him, condensed to its essence.

He replied, "It is all right if I die now. All you disciples, do not waste the important things I've taught you about dharma. In order to protect the vajrayana teachings, all you brothers and sisters, protect your samaya as you would your lives. Practice in mountain retreats and in sealed hermitages. Don't cast aside the recognition within yourselves of the primordially pure, original nature. Resolve once and for all that there is nothing to be seen or searched for other than this emptiness-lucidity with the nature of awareness. Whatever appearances of pleasure and suffering arise, their nature is primordially liberated, so do not sully them with rejection, acceptance, hope, or fear. They are liberated simultaneously with their arising, so give rise to confidence in liberation. In brief, if you are aware that samsara and nirvana are like the front and back of a hand, you are a buddha; if you are unaware of that, you are a sentient being. Therefore don't forget the nature of self-arisen awareness. There is nothing other than this, nothing better than this, to be done."[113]

"Throughout innumerable lives I have, in the presence of victors and their children, repeatedly generated bodhichitta and gathered vast accumulations for the benefit of all beings. I have repeatedly made the aspiration to benefit beings both directly and indirectly, both immediately and ultimately, with my body, my speech, and my mind. Through the power of that I have in the past effortlessly accomplished the benefit of countless beings. Until I reach the essence of awakening, I will never forget my aspiration to establish in omniscience all sentient beings throughout space, and especially the farmers and nomads of north and south, vajra siblings, patrons male and female—all connected to me either positively or negatively. Remember me at the six times of day and night; just through that you will gather the accumulations."

After he had said that and given other final advice, I asked, "Lord, to what realm will you go at your passing? Where should we, your disciples, direct our aspirations? Where will your emanation be born?"

In response to those and similar questions, he said, "Ha, ha! My son, how little you remember! My awareness has mixed with the mind of primordially pure Samantabhadra like the space within a broken vase mixing with all of space. I am not going away, and not coming back. There is no coming or going for me in any direction; there is no center, no up, and no down. What can I say about this? Since the absolute truth of dharmata and the relative truth of dharmas are a unity, there is no one answer to your questions. As I am beyond partiality in every way, it will be like the moon in the sky and its reflections in water. In billions of pure realms I will, with billions of bodies, serve all buddhas, venerate them, attend them, ask them to turn the dharmachakra, retain their teachings with infallible memory, and so on. In impure realms I will in a corresponding way benefit countless beings with bodies that appear like theirs. What is certain is that I have complete control over the display of clouds of emanated lives, like magical illusions, and will continue to manifest them until space is empty.

"For the benefit of those who have been my disciples in this life, I will go to the realm of Sukhavati in the west where I will be born in the center of a lotus and live as a bodhisattva. Therefore those with faith in me should direct their aspirations there; it is certain that the father and the children will be reunited. From there, I will send emanations and further emanations. Especially, there will appear one like the sun who will uphold this seat. Ask the Lord Maitreya, Tai Situ Rinpoche, to find him."

He continued to give boundless final advice, both general and specific, to all of us in common and individually. Finally he composed this song as his final instruction to all his disciples:

> "NAMO GURU. Buddha Vajradhara, embodiment
> of all refuges,
> Peerless father guru—I bow to your feet.

Grant your blessing that the minds
Of my disciples and all beings go to the dharma.

"This old man, Chökyi Senge,
Has inconceivable qualities with which he was born.
I am skilled at fitting in with worldly ways.
I have now revealed the dharmakaya.
All the elaborations of effort and intellect have been
purified in the expanse.
All relative and absolute dharmas have been exhausted
in space.
I, a yogin of space with nothing to do,
Am beyond birth and death in absolute truth.
However, why should I not expose the hidden nature
of the composite?[114]

"Nowadays, at the end of the age of degeneration,
Both central and outlying areas are tormented by war.
Now, when the destruction of the dharmachakra is near,[115]
I have requested the intercession of the victors of the
ten directions.
They have sent their noble mother as their messenger.
She embodies the activity of them all.
In accordance with the commands of the Lord Guru,
the second Buddha,
I have opened wide many doors of interdependent means.
I have prayed for the welfare of all regions.
Now this old man must lay his kindly hopes aside.

"One never knows when this illusion will end,
So all you disciples who depend on me,

Entrust yourselves to the guru and the three jewels.
Don't cling to this life; think of the next.
Live alone on isolated mountains.
Keep the path of generation and completion as the
framework of your lives.
Untie the knot of hope and fear deep within you.
Remain in the fortress of the natural mind.

"All you men and women of this vast land,
Don't talk about how bad the times are
Without seeing how bad your own behavior is!
All of you—powerful and weak—consider yourselves!
Rulers, don't do shameful things.
Subjects, don't agitate improperly.
Don't change your hats, dress, and appearance.
Don't cast aside the deeds of the past.
Maintain the two sanghas as objects of veneration.[116]
Take loving care of your parents and the needy.
Be earnest in benevolence.
Relinquish deception and fakery in thought and deed.
When you are overcome by your enemy, the lord of death,
You will be glad to have no regrets.
Don't be mistaken in your actions; carefully engage
in cause and result.

"Meditate upon your body, appearance-emptiness, as
the body of the noble one.
With your speech recite the six syllables.
With your mind look at the nature of present self-awareness.
Aspire to rebirth in Sukhavati.

"These are this old man's final instructions.
I have never discriminated among those
With whom I have either a good or a bad connection.
I have no attachment to some and aversion to others.
I have said all this with the benevolent wish to help
you all.
Don't forget these things. Keep them in your heart."

Saying that, he filled my mind with the inconceivable secret amrita of his speech, which I received through his boundless kindness and my good fortune. I felt that I could not bear to be parted from him, and repeatedly took the four empowerments. Finally, I left for my home.

That was the third part, the conclusion to the inner and secret autobiography of the lord of the hundred families, the noble guru, Mahavajradhara.

The bhagavat, the splendor of all, the "blood-drinking"
heruka's
Radiant display of "joyous wisdom,"
In the drop of "great bliss," a "blazing vajra" body[117]—
I remember you, lord of all families!

KYE HO! More secret than the secret are your qualities,
Utterly profound and reaching the limits of
the dharmadhatu.
They are way beyond the realm of speech.
They are the inconceivable realm of the victors'
wisdom expanse.

However, the music of your deeds, noble lord,
apparent to us all,
I have described a little in your words.
I am fortunate and delighted,
For your words are medicine, transferring your
wisdom to us.

It is impossible to fully describe the inconceivable
Emanation of a teacher in the realm of those
to be taught.
Without distinction in worthiness, all you touch
Are manifestly freed. Who else has your power?

Your vajra body blazes with the splendid light of compassion.
As soon as it is seen, the darkness of bewildered thoughts
Disappears of itself. One is left in natural self-liberation.
Of your very nature, you liberate through being seen.

Through mastery of the cloud-like wheel of letters,
From the fine vase of your throat, the sambhoghachakra,
Issues secret speech, the melody of nada, and all of it
Brings the miracle of liberation through hearing.

Absolute equality, the spacious expanse of the ground,
Is filled with clear light, the mandala of wisdom and love.
Its thousand rays, blazing with splendid benefit and
bliss, bring to bloom the lotus garden
Of our minds through their touch, which
bestows liberation.

Your wondrous qualities, profound and vast,

Are a canopy woven of garlands of wish-fulfilling
jewels,
Raining down upon us all the siddhis we could ever
wish for.
Those who taste this rain sing in the crazy spontaneity
of their realization.

Peerless guru, you are an actual perfect buddha.
Your deeds, like the activity of all victors,
Are inconceivable. But at the very moment of
recollecting them,
One finds rest in the bed of tranquil bliss, and is
liberated.

KYE HO! Lord of Dharma, sovereign of the hundred
families,
Emperor of siddhas, store of an ocean of profound
treasure,
In your mastery of the wheel of the four activities,
Your splendid light brings benefit and bliss to all beings.

You have never for a moment thought of your own
benefit.
In your vast work for beings and all the teachings,
Through the various means within your activity,
You have worked to help others without respite,
day and night.

Through the miracle of transforming an instant
into an aeon,
The great seal of your inconceivable deeds,

Displayed here as a virtuous spectacle before all
existence and tranquility,
Shows clearly the vast imprint you have left.

Holding the blessed treasury of tantra, agama,
and upadesha,
With perfected experience and realization, with
the complete power of the two wisdoms,
You accomplish the two aims and have mastery
over appearance and existence.
King of teachers, all who think of you do so with faith.

E MA! Your life story is like all space.
The little bee of my intellect with its tiny wings,
Although it wishes to, could never fathom it.
However, through faith and devotion alone,
In the immaculate, great lotus garden of your life
I have had the good fortune to drink sweet nectar,
And, having tasted it, am satisfied.

I present this for the delight of the fortunate.
Its virtue, immaculately pure amrita,
I scatter to the limits of space, without concept.
May the rain of this dedication fall on the whole
of existence,
Filling it with the ripened fruit of peace.

On the summit of the high mountain of the
nine vehicles,
May the divine residence of the holders of the
teachings blaze with splendor.

May the light of the sun and moon of study and practice
Fill the sky in all directions, beautifying the world.

May I carry bound to my head the load
Of the peerless guru's teachings, upholding study
and practice
Through hearing, thinking, and meditating,
Until the end of existence, serving them in the best way.

This illumination of the hidden aspects of the life of the sovereign lord of all families, guru Mahavajradhara, was received by me, as the ambrosia of his speech, during my repeated attendance at his lotus feet. I wrote it down as he spoke, starting in his seventieth year and continuing into his eighty-third year. Having placed through faith the golden flower of this supreme refuge lord's command on my head, on the occasion of the Teacher's turning of the dharmachakra of the four noble truths, in the month Chutö of the Female Earth Sheep Year of the fifteenth cycle,[118] I, Karma Kagyu Tashi, Gyalsay Shenpen Chökyi Drakpa, the least of my guru's disciples, began to edit it, adorning it with a few words of introduction, connection, and conclusion, at Palri Chöying Dzö, the retreat at Dongak Shaydrup Puntsok Targyay Ling, the seat of Dharma Lord Kyodrakpa. However, because of distraction, it remained unfinished.

The guru's son Karma Trinlay Palzang, his son, the realized Trime Loden, and many other holy beings—in particular Gar Choktrul Könchok Tendzin Gyalway Nyugu, the chariot of the great secret teachings—repeatedly bestowed their encouragement. Therefore on a good day in the Wood Rat Year of the fifteenth cycle,[119] I finished it in the Golden Cave of Chapti, the place of accomplishment of the Dharma Lord and his Lady.[120] May it serve to revive the memories of our guru's heart sons, who possess eyes of discernment as wide open as space. I ask that they therefore make any necessary corrections and then disseminate it widely. Through the virtue of this may all beings emulate the life of the glorious guru and achieve the state of supreme liberation.

SARVAMANGALAM

ACKNOWLEDGMENTS

We wish to acknowledge the inspiration of Bardor Tulku Rinpoche, and his kindness in providing the handwritten editon of the Tibetan text translated in this book.

We are also grateful to Lama Tashi Topgyal for his answers to so many questons; to Sally Clay, Jonathan Elwell, and Mary Young for their professional assistance; to Peter Banas and Naomi Schmidt for their technical assistance; to Wendy Harding for both the illustration and thangka painting of Terchen Barway Dorje; to Barbara Majewska for the photograph of the Third Bardor Tulku Rinpoche; and to Bruce Carpenter and Patrick Taylor for their generosity.

Yeshe Gyamtso, Maureen McNicholas, and Peter van Deurzen—KTD Publications

Notes

1. Guru Rinpoche, often called Padmasambhava or Padmakara, is referred to here as indistinguishable from Terchen Barway Dorje.

2. "Father and mother" refers here and elsewhere in this book to Guru Rinpoche and his eminent disciple Yeshe Tsogyal. Barway Dorje was an emanation of Yeshe Tsogyal.

3. Düdül Lingpa is another name given to Barway Dorje by Guru Rinpoche. "Blazing Vajra of Great Bliss" is a translation of the name Dechen Barway Dorje.

4. This refers to Barway Dorje as indistinguishable from the dharmakaya Vajradhara.

5. Guru Rinpoche is called the Second Buddha because he is considered to be the greatest exponent of Buddha Shakyamuni's tantric teachings. The appellation therefore means "like a seond Shakyamuni."

6. The editor's name was Kagyu Tashi.

7. Refers to the *Outer Autobiography*, which has not been translated here.

8. This is a reference to the tantric practice of bringing the karmic winds that cause the appearance and perception of apprehended objects and an apprehending subject into the central channel, causing those appearances and perceptions to cease.

9. For the sake of clarity, when the word *buddha* or its synonyms refer to the historical buddha, Buddha Shakyamuni, or are otherwise used as part of a specific name, they are capitalized here. When these words are used generally or to refer to a state of being, they are not. For the same reason, when the word *guru* is used, as it often is by Tibetans, to refer to Guru Rinpoche, it is capitalized; when it is used to refer to others it is not. When the term *heruka* is used as a proper name it is capitalized, and when used to refer to a type of deity or yogin it is not.

10. The six elements are earth, fire, water, air, space, and cognition.

11. Our Teacher refers here to Buddha Shakyamuni.

12. Pramodhavajra is Sanskrit for Garab Dorje [Tib.]

13. Tantras, agamas, and upadeshas are three sources of vajrayana tradition. Often they correspond to mahayoga, anuyoga, and atiyoga respectively, although each of these vehicles also contains all three. It is sometimes explained, "Tantras are what the Buddha taught; agamas are what the bodhisattvas compiled; and upadeshas are what the vidyadharas presented."

14. Changlochen is the realm of Vajrapani.

15. Here and elsewhere, "the great revealer of treasure," *terchen* in Tibetan, refers to Chokgyur Lingpa. The title is also accorded to Barway Dorje, and Kagyu Tashi uses it to refer to him, but Barway Dorje only uses it to refer to his guru. This title is given to treasure revealers, tertöns, who have discovered the three principal types of terma: Gurusadhana, Great Compassion, and Great Perfection.

16. *Viras* means "heroes," male deities.

17. The five wheels of ornament are body, speech, mind, qualities, and activity.

18. Either standard refers to mundane or dharmic.

19. Mönmo Tashi Khyidren was one of Guru Rinpoche's five principal consorts.

20. 1836.

21. Uddiyana Vajradhara is a form of Guru Rinpoche.

22. Mandarava is Guru Rinpoche's great Indian disciple.

23. Barway Dorje was recognized as a tulku of Surmang Monastery. Because his father was a leader of the Rakshul region, Barway Dorje was known as "Rakshul Tulku." Abbreviated to "Raktrul," this also became the informal name of the monastery he founded.

24. Cotton dharma is a ceremony in which yogins accomplished in the chandali practice demonstrate their control over body temperature by wearing and drying wet cotton sheets in extremely cold weather.

25. Here and elsewhere in this book Barway Dorje frankly describes his experiences of the completion stage. Here he is describing experiences associated with chandali, the first of the Six Dharmas of Naropa.

26. Padma Tenkyong, also called Padma Tensung here, is a protector of Palpung Monastery.

27. Speedy messengers refers to dakinis as bringers of realization.

28. It is customary for treasure revealers to marry, although there have been exceptions to this.

29. Pratimoksha, bodhisattva, and samaya vows.

30. *Terchen* means "great revealer of treasure." Here as elsewhere in this book, Barway Dorje uses it to refer to Chokgyur Dechen Lingpa; Kagyu Tashi, the editor of the autobiography, uses it to refer to Barway Dorje.

31. *Tukdrup Barchay Kunsel, The Sadhana Of The Guru's Mind Which*

Dispels All Obstacles, is perhaps the most famous of Chokgyur Lingpa's thirty-eight principal treasures.

32. The two Manjushri protectors are Jamyang Khyentse Wangpo and Jamgön Lodrö Thaye.

33. Vajrachanda is a wrathful form of Vajrapani, here also a form of Guru Rinpoche.

34. 1862. As Trinlay Palzang was Barway Dorje's first son, the year given in the text for the birth of his second son, 1852, appears to be an error.

35. "Mature awareness" refers to the third of the four levels of Great Perfection realization.

36. In some contexts Barway Dorje appears to use "north and south" to mean "east and west," eastern and central Tibet. At other times it appears to refer to northern and southern parts of eastern Tibet.

37. Another treasure of Chokgyur Lingpa. The two "Jamgöns" are the two "Manjushri Protectors."

38. Treasure punctuation refers to a mark consisting of two circles, one above the other, with a crescent between them that is used to seal and protect the integrity of treasure texts. It is put at the end of every line of verse and wherever punctuation is needed in prose.

39. The three aspects are doer, deed, and doing. Sometimes they are explained as doer, deed, and beneficiary or beneficiaries of the deed; and sometimes as giver, gift, and recipient.

40. A conventional isolate is a concept employed to distinguish a thing from all that is not that thing.

41. Severance is the renowned tradition of Machik Lapdrön. As it is a method for the direct severance of fixation on a self, its practice is characterized by the overcoming of fear even in the midst of upheaval.

42. A reversal practice is one done to avert disaster; Kimkams are protectors in the retinue of wrathful deities such as Yamantaka.

43. Six-syllables refers to OM MANI PADME HUM, the mantra of Avalokiteshvara.

44. 1852, the Water Rat Year, appears to be incorrect. The correct year may be 1864, the Wood Rat Year.

45. *The Pride of Nupchen* is a recollection discovery of Chokgyur Lingpa. There is also a treasure with the same name that was revealed by Barway Dorje.

46. Sangngak Choling is the seat of the Drukchen Rinpoche, the head of the Drukpa Kagyu.

47. Lopas are the people who inhabit the region shared by Tibet and Assam.

48. Dakinis may be connate, mantra-born, or place-born.

49. The Earth Snake Year, 1869.

50. Lest the reader be shocked by the brevity of this into mistaking it as callousness, it should be mentioned that, in his *Outer Autobiography,* Barway Dorje describes his grief at the loss of his teacher at length. Since the *Inner Autobiography* was intended to be primarily a record of visions and discoveries, he does not describe his feelings here.

51. The Supreme Sons are activity emanations of Vajrakumara.

52. In general, atsara, apparently derived from acharya, means a "mendicant yogin." It is also the name of a specific protector.

53. A golden drink is a ritual libation containing gold powder.

54. The four impossibilities are the child of a childless woman, the horns of a rabbit, the hair of a tortoise, and a flower growing in the sky.

Since it was believed that elephants lack saliva, the saliva of elephants could be considered one as well.

55. The eight qualities of mastery are subtle form, visible form, lightness, all-pervasiveness, perfect attainment, utter clarity, stability, and the acquisition of all that is desired.

56. Five-fold degeneration refers to degenerations of beings, kleshas, views, lifespan, and time.

57. "According to your wishes" is *Yishin;* "jewel" is *Norbu.* This is a play on the name of the teacher to whom the song was addressed.

58. This disease, white pox, is explained as a less virulent but still potentially life-threatening ailment related to smallpox, which is called the black pox. Although the white pox has been thought to refer to chicken pox, its evident virulence and the assertion that it creates an immunity to smallpox appear to contradict that.

59. "Seated like Maitreya" means to be seated as we would sit in a chair.

60. "The Fathers and Sons" refers to the head of a great lineage and his regents, who will in turn serve as his teachers in his next life. For example, in the case of the Karma Kamtsang Kagyu this term refers to His Holiness the Gyalwa Karmapa and his principal teachers.

61. The past war refers to a conflict between the eastern Tibetan kingdoms and China.

62. *The Padma Katang* is the biography of Guru Rinpoche revealed by Orgyen Lingpa, often read aloud as a devotional exercise.

63. The Five Forms of the Great King refers to the five emanations of the protector Pehar.

64. It is believed that one inherits from one's parents a connection with various devas.

65. The Bird Year is probably 1885; possibly 1873. Since, in the next

section, Barway Dorje refers to events in his late fifties, in the last decade of the nineteenth century, the Bird Year referred to here is most likely 1885.

66. The Pig Year is probably 1887; possibly 1875.

67. A ceremony conducted by a solitary male practitioner.

68. The eye of the land is the most auspicious site for construction.

69. Dragon Year refers to either 1892 or 1904. If we presume that this section follows the previous ones sequentially, 1904 is more likely.

70. A joy swirl is a circular design composed of three or more sections coiled around one another. It represents great bliss.

71. According to most sources, four of the thousand buddhas of this aeon have already appeared, Buddha Shakyamuni being the fourth of these. However, some sources indicate that there are other buddhas, not numbered among the thousand, who appear in between, bringing the number of buddhas who have appeared in this aeon up to seven.

72. Teurang, like tsen and nyen, are a type of non-human being. They are usually invisible, and are capable of being both helpful and spiteful. We use the term *spirit* to refer to all such beings in English, but they perceive themselves as possessing bodies, and, as is mentioned throughout this book, are sometimes seen by humans as well.

73. The Shvanas are protectors of the Vajrakila mandala.

74. Gingkaras are protectors of the Vajrakila mandala and others.

75. Akanishtha is the highest pure realm. Here it is identified with Blazing Mountains of Fire, the principal and highest wrathful pure realm.

76. Taksham Nüden Dorje is a treasure revealer of the 17th century.

77. Sangye Wön is the renowned founder of Riwoche Monastery.

78. In the treasures of Barway Dorje, the nine vidyadharas are the eight associated with the eight dispensations from the mandala of *The Sugatas' Assembly* with the addition of Pramodhavajra, associated in this context with Vajrasattva.

79. 1913.

80. 1914. Barway Dorje's monastery, known as "Raktrul Monastery" after its founder, still exists.

81. Matiratna refers to Trungmase Lodrö Rinchen.

82. The eight classes are the eight principal types of what are generally called "spirits."

83. A thread-cross is an offering connected with the removal of impediments.

84. Barway Dorje was the reincarnation of the Dharma Lord of Kyodrak, Sönam Zangpo.

85. The twenty-five sacred places referred to so often in this book were revealed by Chokgyur Lingpa, and are all in eastern Tibet. There is a similar list of 100 sacred places in central Tibet.

86. Kirtidhvaja is Drakpa Gyaltsen; Mati and Punya are Lodrö Rinchen and Sönam Zangpo respectively.

87. The duration of the Buddha's teaching is divided into five-hundred year periods, each more degenerate than the previous one.

88. *The Sutra of the Vast Assembly* is a tantra of the anuyoga.

89. Alloy goddesses are deities depicted with the bodies of goddesses and the heads of various animals. They represent the qualities associated with those animals. Since they combine the compassion of the male principal of their mandala and the discernment of the female principal they are an alloy of these, like something made from a mixture of gold and silver.

90. A Stupa of Many Auspicious Doors is one of the eight principal types of stupa. It represents the variety of the Buddha's teachings, all of them leading ultimately to the same awakening.

91. The two sites are the White Rock of Chapti and the Dakinis' Throne.

92. The visions described here are those that arise through the practice of leapover, a unique feature of the Great Perfection teachings. The kila of awareness is one of the "four penetrations" that form the complete path according to the *Vajrakilatantras.*

93. The name of the emanation is not stated here.

94. Vajradhara, here referred to as Mahavajradhara, is called the sixth buddha because he embodies all five buddha families.

95. Düdül Lingpa is another name given to Barway Dorje by Guru Rinpoche. It means "Treasure Revealer Who Subdues Mara."

96. *Jampal Dorje Tritsum* is another of Barway Dorje's names. It means "Manjushrivajra Noble Throne."

97. Chusöl Tokden is the renowned Chusöl Yonten Gyamtso associated with Goche Monastery in the former Kingdom of Nangchen.

98. Eating, sleeping, and excreting.

99. The twenty-eight Ishvaras are female deities who appear in many wrathful mandalas. The nine moods comprise the demeanor of wrathful deities. They are often called "the nine moods of dance," as the depiction of them is considered one of the aims of dance, drama, and music. They are: the erotic, heroic, and unpleasant (the three moods of body); violence, laughter, and the terrifying (the three moods of speech); and compassion, rage, and tranquility (the three moods of mind).

100. The year of conflict referred to is 1856.

101. The next Fire Dragon Year was 1916.

102. The three gates to liberation are emptiness, absence of characteristics, and absence of aspiration. These correspond to ground, path, and result respectively.

103. The sixteen elders are sixteen disciples of Buddha Shakyamuni entrusted by him with the custody of his teachings. They are all arhats and are believed to be still alive.

104. Three gatherings refers to the spontaneous gathering of dakinis, people, and food.

105. Here Barway Dorje addresses Kalzang, "Good Fortune," as "Kalpika," a Sanskrit version of her name.

106. These events occurred in the year following the first performance of *The Great Feast Dance.* Since it was first performed in 1916, this would have been in the year 1917. It is generally accepted that Barway Dorje passed away in 1920. This autobiography was first edited in 1919, apparently before Barway Dorje's passing. Kagyu Tashi writes that the biography extends to his teacher's eighty-third year, 1919.

107. This appears to refer to the third yearly performance of the dance, and therefore to the year 1918.

108. Practicing dharma in accord with dharma means to practice with the motivation of bodhichitta.

109. The Male Earth Horse Year was 1918.

110. Lord guru here refers to Terchen Barway Dorje.

111. The "exhaustion of intellect and dharmas" is the fourth and final level of Great Perfection realization.

112. No meditation is the fourth and final yoga of mahamudra.

113. This is instruction on Pramodhavajra's *Three Words That Hit the Point*: direct recognition within oneself, single and final resolution, and the establishment of the confidence of realization.

114. His reference to exposing the hidden nature of the composite means that he is demonstrating death as a lesson to others.

115. This appears to predict the invasion of 1950.

116. The monastic sangha and the sangha of tantrikas.

117. The words in quotation marks are a translation of the name Traktung Dechen Barway Dorje.

118. 1919.

119. 1924.

120. Dharma Lord and his Lady refers to Chöje Sönam Zangpo and his consort.

The Third Barway Dorje Tulku Rinpoche

Kunzang Palchen Ling

The Third Barway Dorje Tulku Rinpoche, Karma Drupgyü Tenpay Nyima, teaches the treasures of Terchen Barway Dorje at Kunzang Palchen Ling, All-Good Great Splendor Park, in Red Hook, New York. Those interested in finding out more about Rinpoche's teachings and activity, or in supporting Raktrul Monastery in Eastern Tibet, may contact:

Kunzang Palchen Ling
Red Hook, New York
www.Kunzang.org

Karma Triyana Dharmachakra

Karma Triyana Dharmachakra (KTD) is the North America seat of His Holiness the Gyalwa Karmapa, and under the spiritual guidance and protection of His Holiness Ogyen Trinley Dorje, the Seventeenth Gyalwa Karmapa, is devoted to the authentic representation of the Kagyu lineage of Tibetan Buddhism.

For information regarding KTD, including our current schedule, or for information regarding our affiliate centers, Karma Thegsum Choling (KTC), located both in the United States and internationally, contact us using the information below.

Karma Triyana Dharmachakra
335 Meads Mountain Road
Woodstock, NY, 12498 USA
845 679 5906 ext. 10
www.kagyu.org
KTC Coordinator: 845 679 5701
ktc@kagyu.org

KTD Publications

GATHERING THE GARLANDS OF THE GURUS' PRECIOUS TEACHINGS

KTD Publications, a part of Karma Triyana Dharmachakra, is a not-for-profit publisher established with the purpose of facilitating the projects and activities manifesting from His Holiness's inspiration and blessings. We are dedicated to gathering the garlands of precious teachings and producing fine-quality books.

We invite you to join KTD Publications in facilitating the activities of His Holiness Karmapa and fulfilling the wishes of Khenpo Karthar Rinpoche and Bardor Tulku Rinpoche. If you would like to sponsor a book or make a donation to KTD Publications, please contact us using the information below. All contributions are tax-deductible.

KTD Publications
335 Meads Mountain Road
Woodstock, NY, 12498 USA
Telephone: 845 679 5906 ext. 37
www.KTDPublications.org